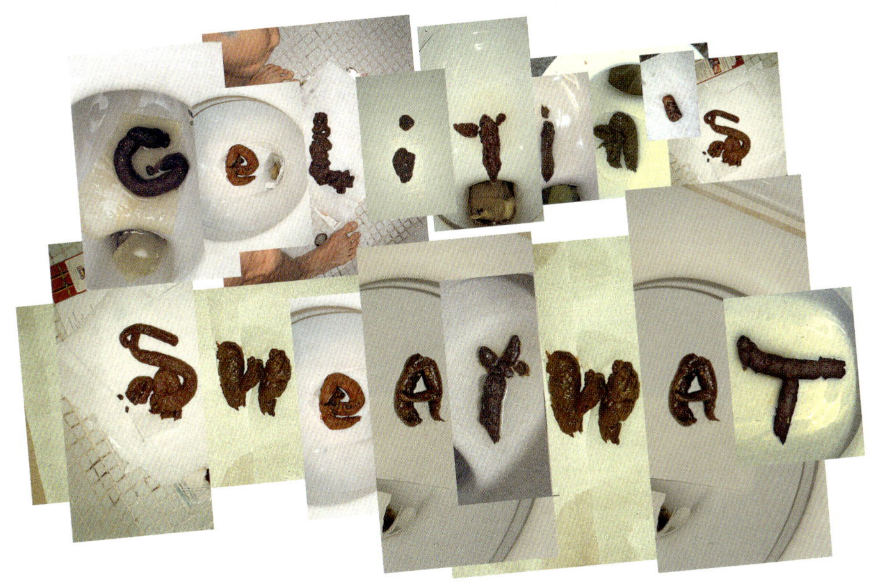


GOLiTIAS
SWeATWAT

AF478983

**Gelitin's Sweatwat**
Service complet
October 17 – October 21, 2005
From 6pm until 11pm
Exhibition: October 22 – November 26, 2005

Gagosian Gallery
6 – 24 Britannia Street
London WC1X9JD
UK

SWEATWAT . . Once a Noun, now a Verb
Text by Cerith Wyn Evans

Puddle Trouble: *Sweatwat* at King's Cross
Text by Claire Bishop

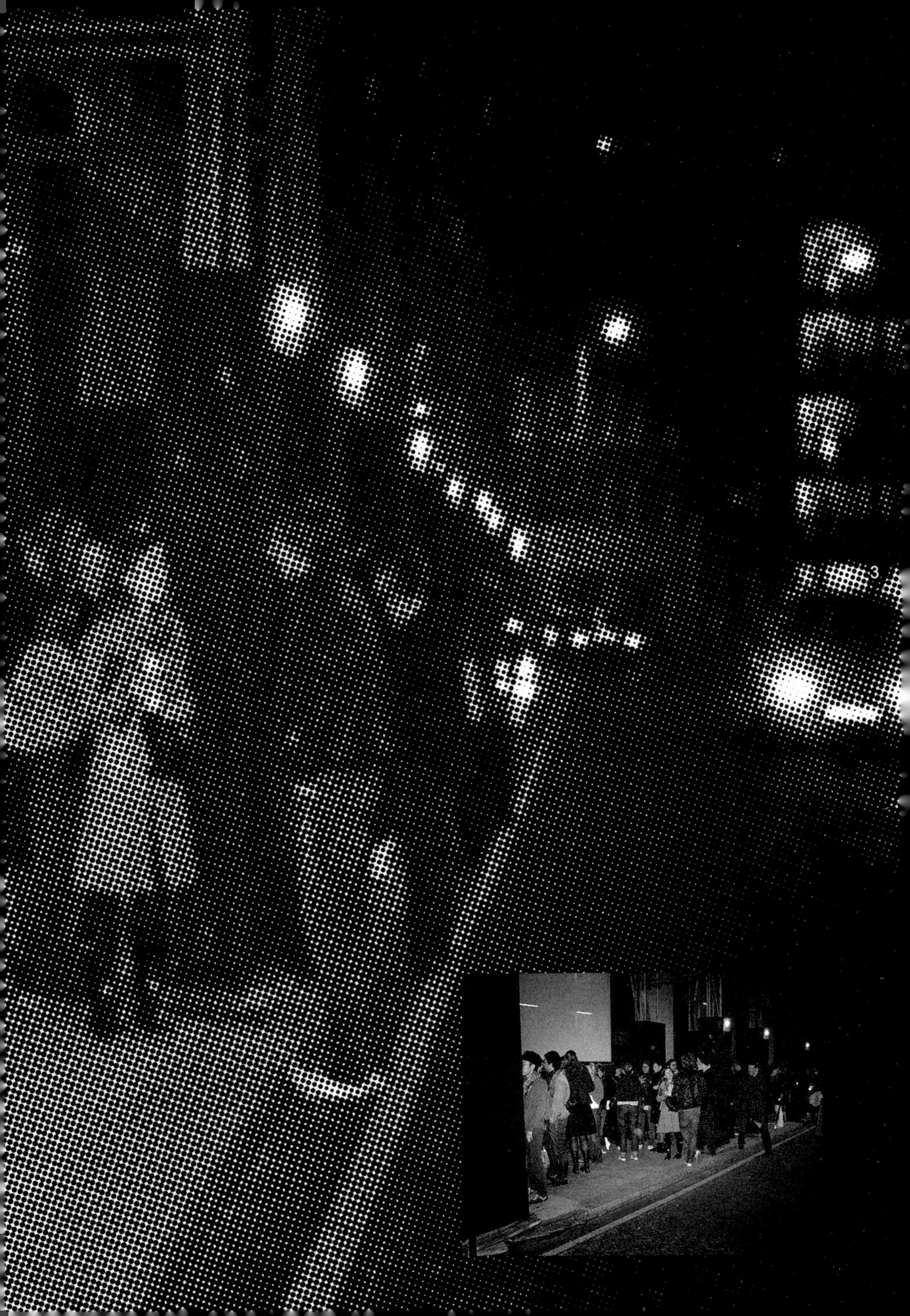

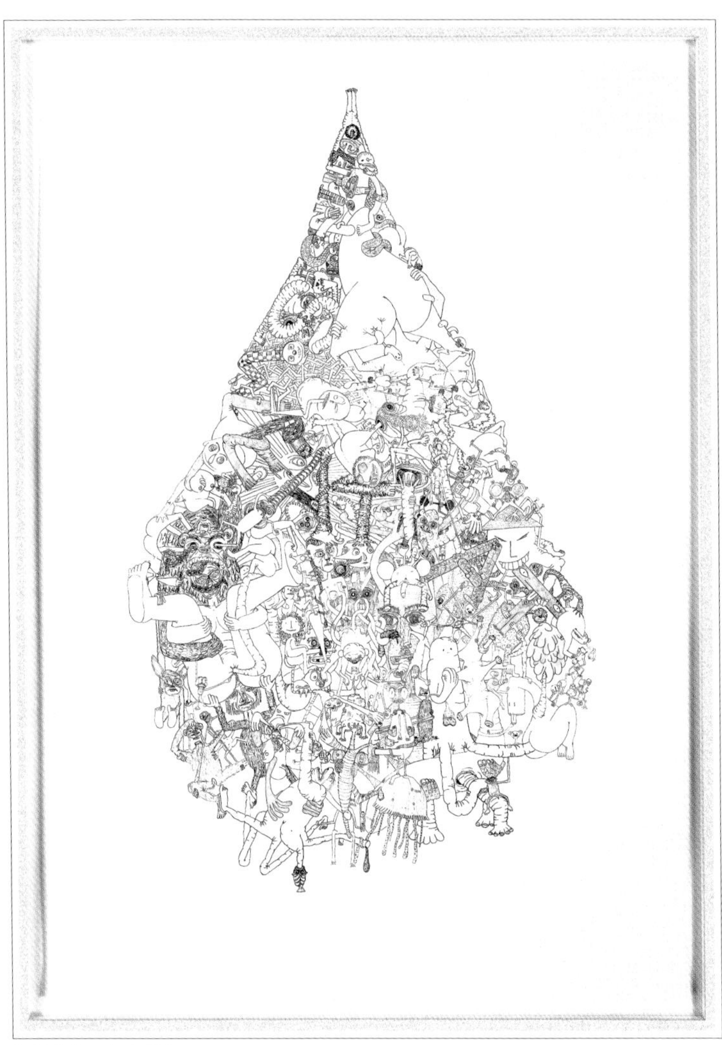

*Gelitin's Sweatwat*, 2005
pencil on paper
39 1/2 x 27 1/2 inches
(100.2 x 70.2 cm)

# DISCLAIMER

### GELITIN's *SWEATWAT*

The installation which you are about to enter involves you climbing on ladders, crawling, darkness, enclosed spaces and conditions which may be wet, damp and/or dirty.

If you suffer from or may suffer from any condition mental or physical which might adversely affect your enjoyment of the installation or might expose you to harm or distress, or if you do not wish to risk damaging or getting your clothes or personal belongings wet, damp or dirty then do not enter the *Sweatwat.*

If, notwithstanding all the above, you still wish to view and enter the installation please carefully read the disclaimer below before signing and dating it to show your acceptance of the terms.

In consideration of the Gagosian Gallery of London LLC ("Gagosian Gallery") and Gelitin allowing me to enter the Installation *Sweatwat.*

1.  I acknowledge and agree that in entering and viewing the Installation I will be required to participate in physical activity and exertion, including but not limited to, crawling, climbing and entering spaces that may be small, confined, dark, wet and/or dirty.

2.  I warrant that I am physically and mentally capable of viewing and entering the Installation and acknowledge and agree that whilst in the Installation my clothing and other personal items may be damaged or become wet or dirty.

3.  I agree that the Gagosian Gallery (including its officers and employees) and Gelitin, will not be liable for any injury or illness that I may suffer (or the consequences of any injury or illness) or for any damage or soiling (temporary or permanent) to my clothing and personal belongings that may occur as a result of my viewing and entering the Installation. I further acknowledge that the Gagosian Gallery (including its officers and employees) and Gelitin will not be liable for any indirect or consequential loss I may suffer as a result of my viewing and/or entering the installation.

4.  Nothing in this Disclaimer shall exclude or limit the liability of the Gagosian Gallery or Gelitin for death or personal injury caused by the negligence of Gagosian Gallery, or for any matter for which it would be illegal for the Gagosian Gallery or Gelitin to exclude or attempt to exclude its liability.

5.  I confirm that I am 18 or over and agree not to smoke in the Gagosian Gallery.

I confirm my acceptance of the above terms: Frank P Gehry (Print Name and Address)

(Signature)

18/10/05 (Date)

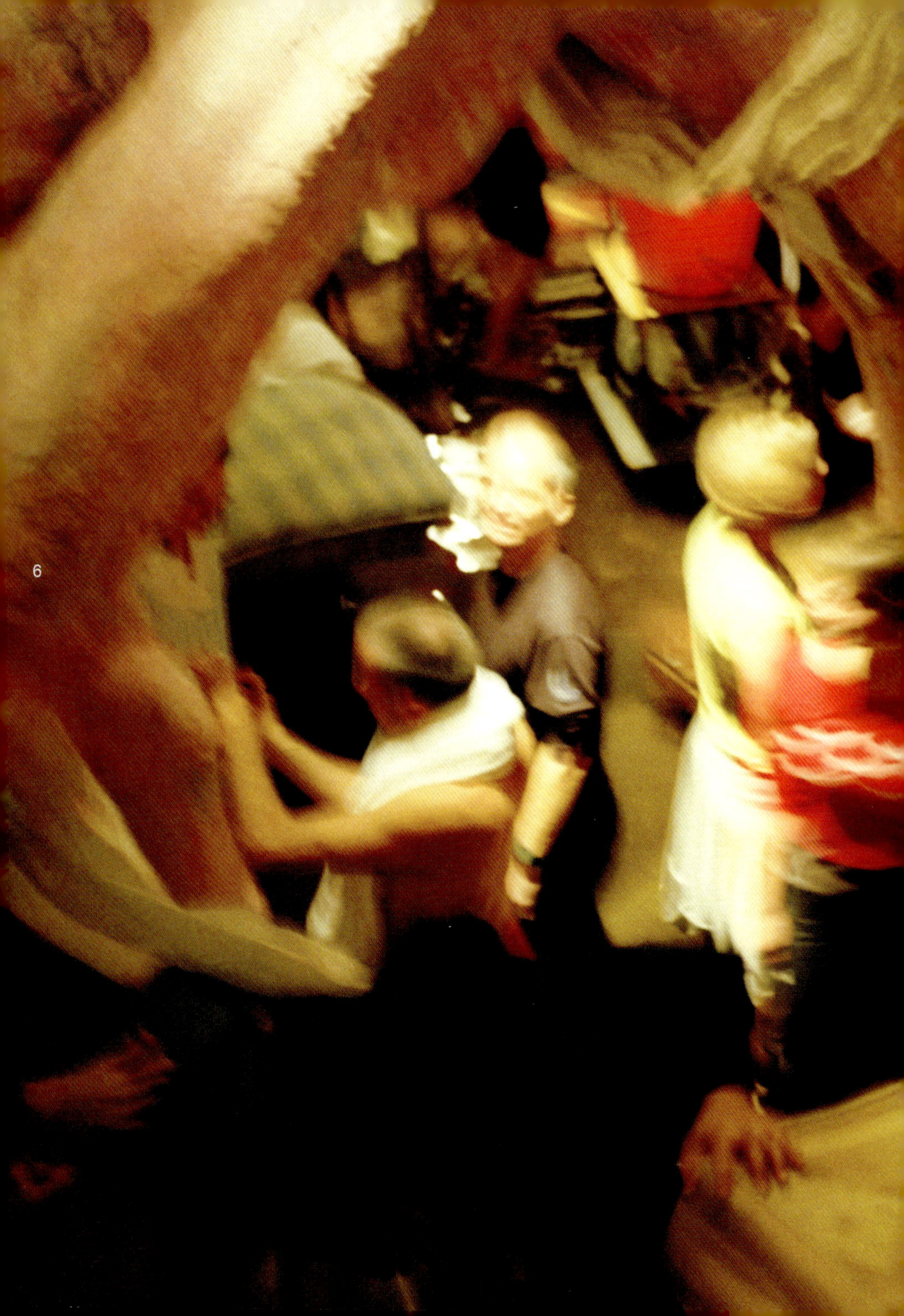

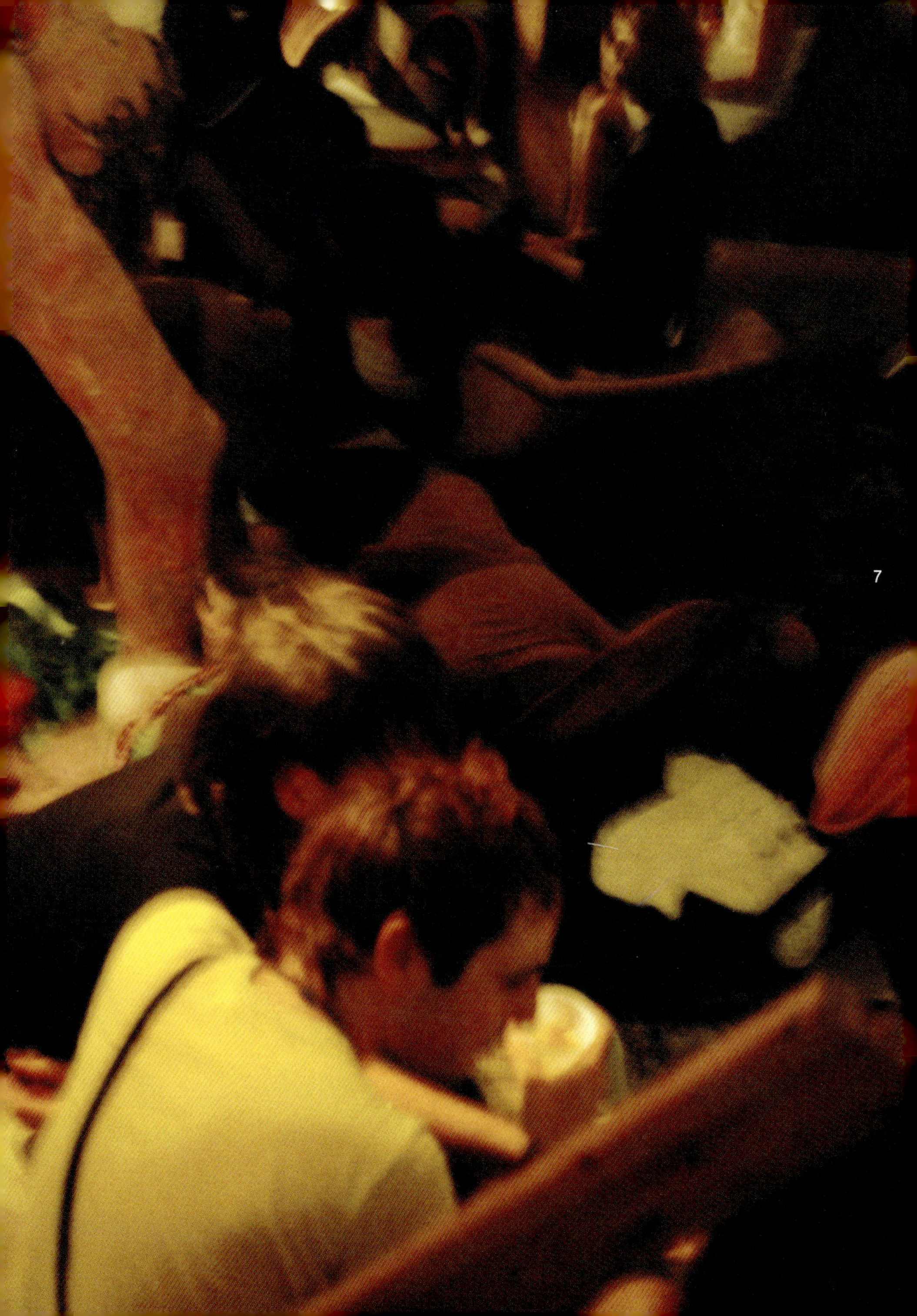

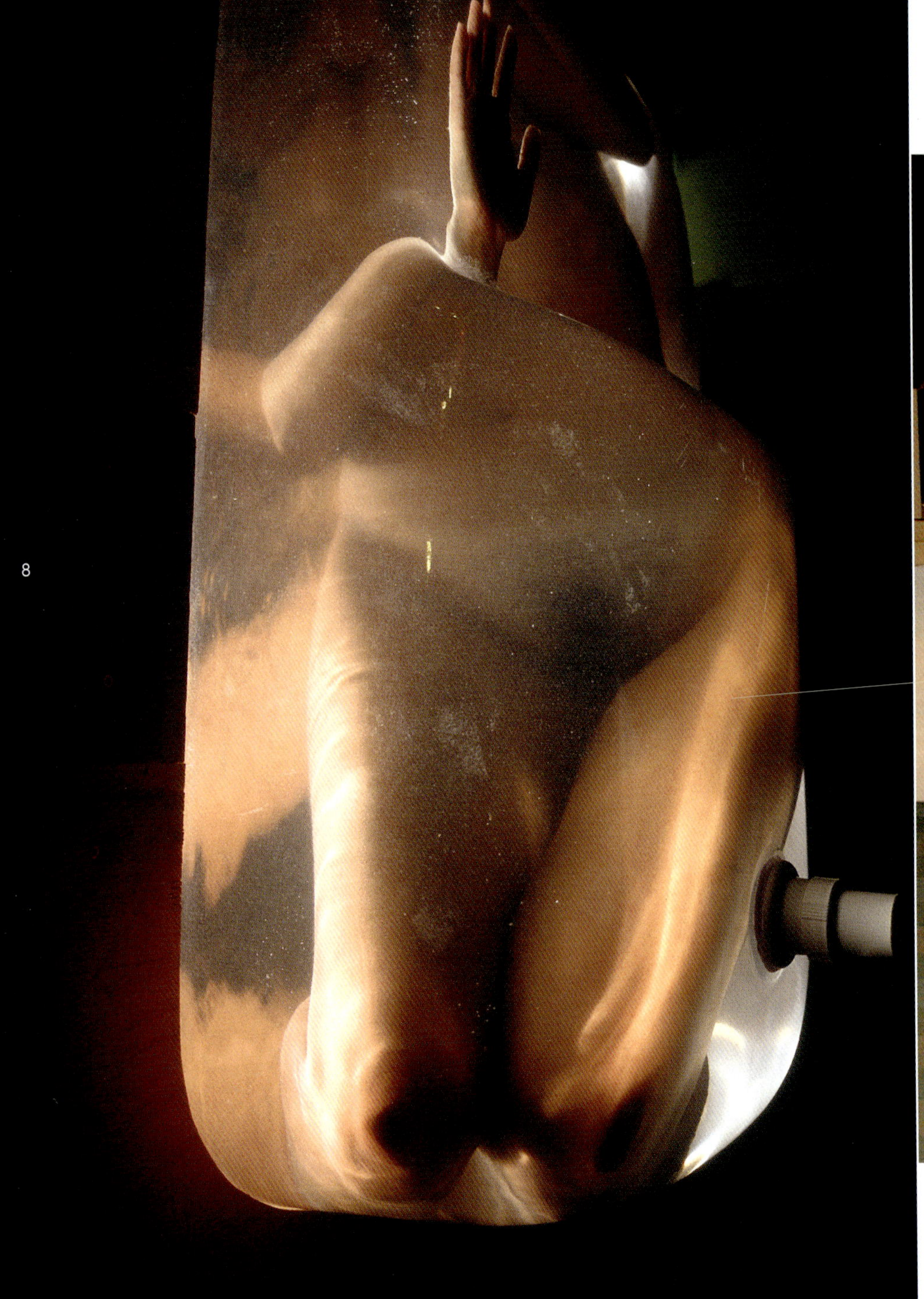

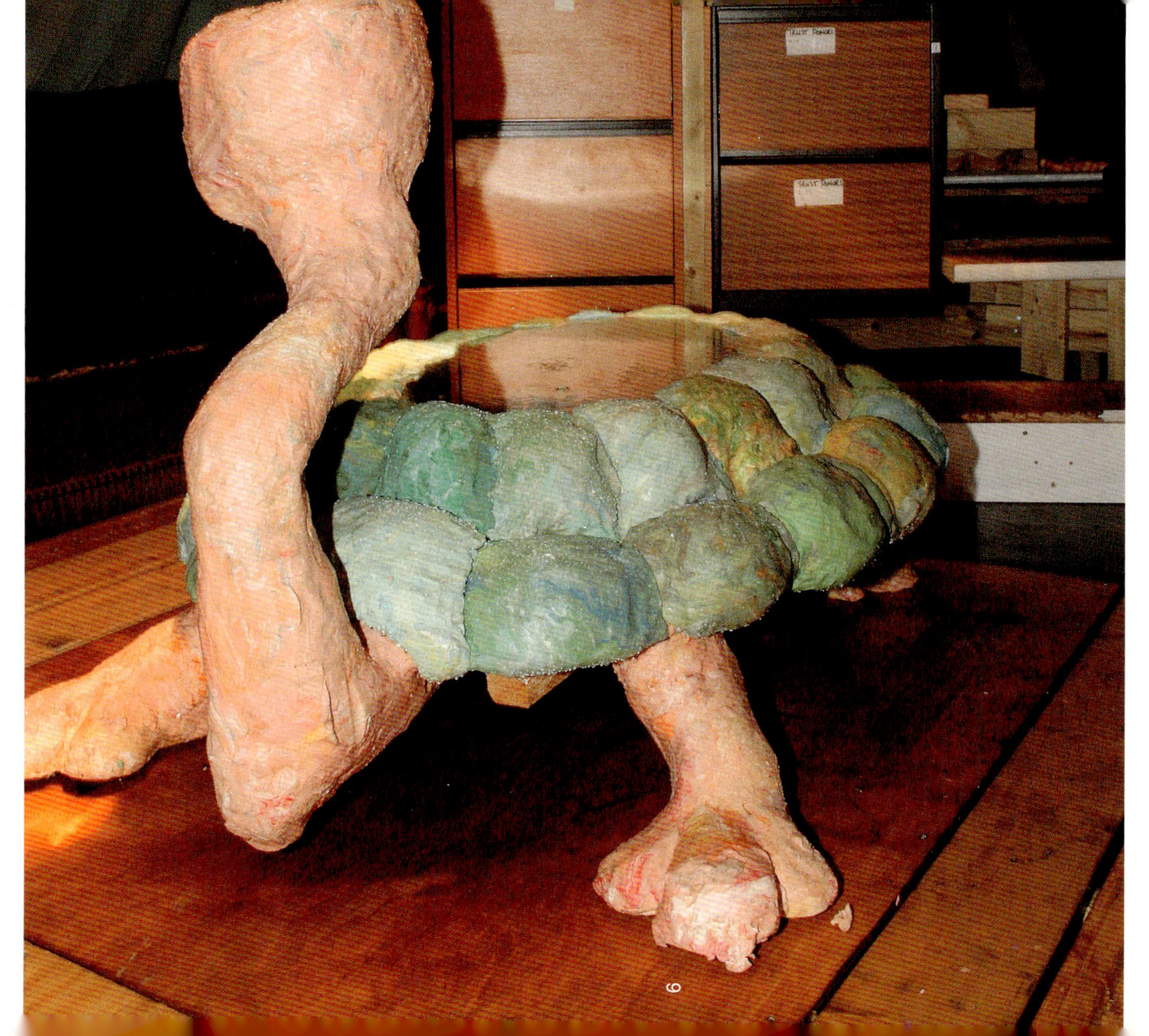

10

…
Noun:
A name, or something like one.
e.g., Gagossian

Verb:
An action, that which is performed.
e.g., "I pissed in the public Swimming Pool"


"…
So, no anecdotes of Production…
Just pillow talk.
And a watery aspect, here we engaged in a
liquid economy, an exchange…dank, permeable
body;
A little stab at happiness.

And the terms and conditions occasion the
radical staging of a threshold.
Generous to a fault.

Let's take it to the bridge…
Threshold.
The threshold (here both temperament and
temperature) occasions the profundity of the
surface…

An economy we share under these conditions
which allow us to sweat together, a community
of liquid exchange; a flow…
And our guiding light we agree is a distant star
whose name is 'Intimacy26'…
Let us go 'Star-Bathing' "

The threshold is the node which separates two
opposing worlds, the interior and the open air.
The cold and the warm, the light and the shade.
To cross a threshold is thus to traverse a zone
of danger where invisible but real battles are
fought out.

As long as the door is closed, all is well. To
open it is a serious matter; it is to unleash two
hordes, one against the other, it is to risk being
caught up in the fray. Far from being a conven-
ience, the door is a terrible instrument which
must be made use of only knowingly and
according to the proper rites, and which must
be surrounded by every magical protection.

These precautions are innumerable: a
horseshoe, a consecrated sprig of box-tree, a
painting of Saint Sebastian surrounded with
formulae, an animal sacrificed on the threshold,
corpses of enemies buried standing erect…

In east Africa the most dangerous moment
of the day is the opening of the door in the
morning. In effect, all night the house has been
closed; it has been, as it were, isolated from the
world, from the open air, from the cold, from the
light. The door has been the thoroughly water-
tight lock-gate that has dammed up the threshold. One will therefore open it with an infinity of
precautions, slowly, keeping behind it, above all
avoiding displacing the air. When it is fully open,
one will spit into the gaping opening, at the
same time pronouncing words of appeasement,
and finally, with the greatest calm, one will cross
the threshold, looking before oneself.

The same movements are observed by the
visitor when he presents himself to the house-
hold in the early morning. However, he will avoid
any complications by not arriving until very late,
when the door will already have been opened
and contact established.

In superior civilisations the doormat has not
been created solely to slow the crossing of the
threshold and permit the visitor to collect his
thoughts. It plays a far more important role;
when the tradesman's representative presents
himself at the door of an important client, he
wipes his feet all the more ostentatiously on the
mat at the door if the house be imposing, and
that even in dry weather. Conversely, in muddy
weather, it is properly polite to say to an hon-
oured visitor who is endeavouring to remove the
mud from his boots: "Oh, I say, please don't
bother." The assiduity one employs in freeing
the stranger from this obligation is in direct ratio
to the respect one has for him.

This goes to show that the threshold, that is
to say the doormat, of which it is the visible
sign, is indeed a thing of dread, because there
one must manifest or cast aside one's qualities,
because there it is necessary to register,
forcibly or with levity, the rank one occupies in
society. The ways of 'conducting' a story offer
a very rich field for the analysis of spatiality.
Among the questions that depend on it, we
should distinguish those that concern dimensions (extensionality), orientation (vectorality),
affinity (homographies), etc. I stress only a few
of its aspects that have to do with delimitation
itself, the primary and literally "fundamental"
question: it is the partition of space that struc-
tures it. Everything refers in fact to this differen-
tiation which makes possible the isolation and
interplay of distinct spaces. From the distinction
that separates a subject from its exteriority to

the distinctions that localize objects, from the home (constituted on the basis of the wall) to the journey (constituted on the basis of a geographical "elsewhere" or a cosmological "beyond"), from the functioning of the urban network to that of the rural landscape, there is no spatiality that is not organized by the determination of frontiers.

In this organization, the story plays a decisive role. It "describes," to be sure. But "every description is more than a fixation," it is "a culturally creative act." It even has distributive power and performative force (it does what it says) when an ensemble of circumstances is brought together. SWEATWAT, then it founds spaces. Reciprocally, where stories are disappearing (or else are being reduced to museographical objects), there is a loss of space: deprived of narrations (as one sees it happen in both the city and the countryside), the group or the individual regresses toward the disquieting, fatalistic experience of a formless, indistinct, and nocturnal totality. By considering the role of stories in delimitation, one can see that the primary function is to authorize the establishment, displacement or transcendence of limits, and as a consequence, to set in opposition, within the closed field of discourse, two movements that intersect (setting and transgressing limits) in such a way as to make the story a sort of "crossword" decoding stencil (a dynamic partitioning of space) whose essential narrative figures seem to be the frontier and the bridge.

1. Creating a theatre of actions. The story's first function is to authorize, or more exactly, to found. Strictly speaking, this function is not lawful, that is, related to laws or judgment. It depends…

The ritual is a foundation. It "provides space" for the actions that will be undertaken; it "creates a field" which serves as their "base" and their "theatre."

Did you ever read, *I Sing the Body Electric* by Walt Whitman? And do you remember the horizon that it revealed?
If not, break away from these words now.
I'm sure you can find it on the Internet……
Or take a walk to the library or bookshop,
Take care to appreciate the way the light falls on your journey.

Read it diligently with respect to the phantom voice, the phantoms you might project invoking the objects of your love…and miracle of miracles…the recognition that in some intractable way the feeling is mutual.

"Gelitin"
…the Artists formerly known as Prince…
(and how touching the anecdotes that abound around the exchange of a vowel)
an *I* for an *a*

"In Course of Arrangement…
Exhibit Temporarily Removed, We are under Construction"

And again, many words whose prefix begin with Trans…
Apply…
List them…
As I attempt here in their numerable or innumerable forms.

So, "SWEATWAT"…a wordplay, and a play in worlds.

Laughter here becomes scale, and the social contract so passionately and delicately constructed, becomes
Engaged.

We are engaged.
Stranger to Professional.
Here all of us together…
"Us," that tea bag of a word, which steeps in the conditional.
How are we to name, to describe that which I see from my place, that lived by another which yet for me is not nothing since I have come to believe in the other- and that which furthermore concerns me myself, since it is there as another's view upon me?
Here is this well-known countenance, these modulations of voice, whose style is as familiar to me as myself.
Perhaps in many moments here the other is for me reduced to a spectacle, which can be a charm…

And circus logic obeys.
Its protocols acknowledged yet…

Now what if the voice alters? What if the
unwanted should appear in the score of the
dialogue, or on the contrary, should a response
respond too well to what I thought without really
having said it – and suddenly there breaks forth
the evidence that out there also, minute by
minute, life is being lived: somewhere behind
those eyes, behind those gestures (Gelitin,
Master Carpenters)…or rather before them,
coming from I know what double ground of
space, another private world shows through,
through the fabric of my own and for these
moments I live in it.
Pleasure Garden: SWEATWAT
And a Theatregarden Bestiarum

Weave a circle 'round him thrice,
His flaming hair, his caves ice,
For he on honeydew hath fed and drunk the
milk of Paradise'

Some Practical Considerations: –
And the Dependence of the Art World Economy
on the Circulation of energy on the Earth…
When it is necessary to change an automobile
tyre, open an abscess or plough a vineyard, it is
easy to manage a quite limited operation. The
elements on which the action is brought to bear
are not completely isolated from the rest of the
world, but it is possible to act on them as if it
were.

One can complete the operation without once
needing to consider the whole, of which the
tyre, the abscess or the…

So, you, my boys Gelitin, do you remember?
I'll call you: – Wolfgang…Florian…Tobias, and
Ali

Send a postcard.

My Dear……We flooded the gallery, it was hard
at first, but the technicians got into it eventually
'cause they realised it wasn't Art, as they knew
it…
Still we had a marvellous time…and compro-
mise was entertained again as usual.
Yours,
Gelitin xxx

The margins of doubt.

Good Morning, Happy Birthday!
SWEATWAT?
YES…

What?
You Heard.
It's called "SWEATWAT"
You can take the courtesy limousine from the
Frieze Art Fair…
"They're from Vienna"

Alphabet of Shit.

Abc…déjà vu.
It is vain to consider, in the appearance of
things, only the intelligible signs that allow the
various elements to be distinguished from each
other.

 John Cage once said…
"Anything Goes but, Anything Goes"

Gelitin.
They are by example…

And the prospect is all yours for the taking…

When were you last so much in love with now?

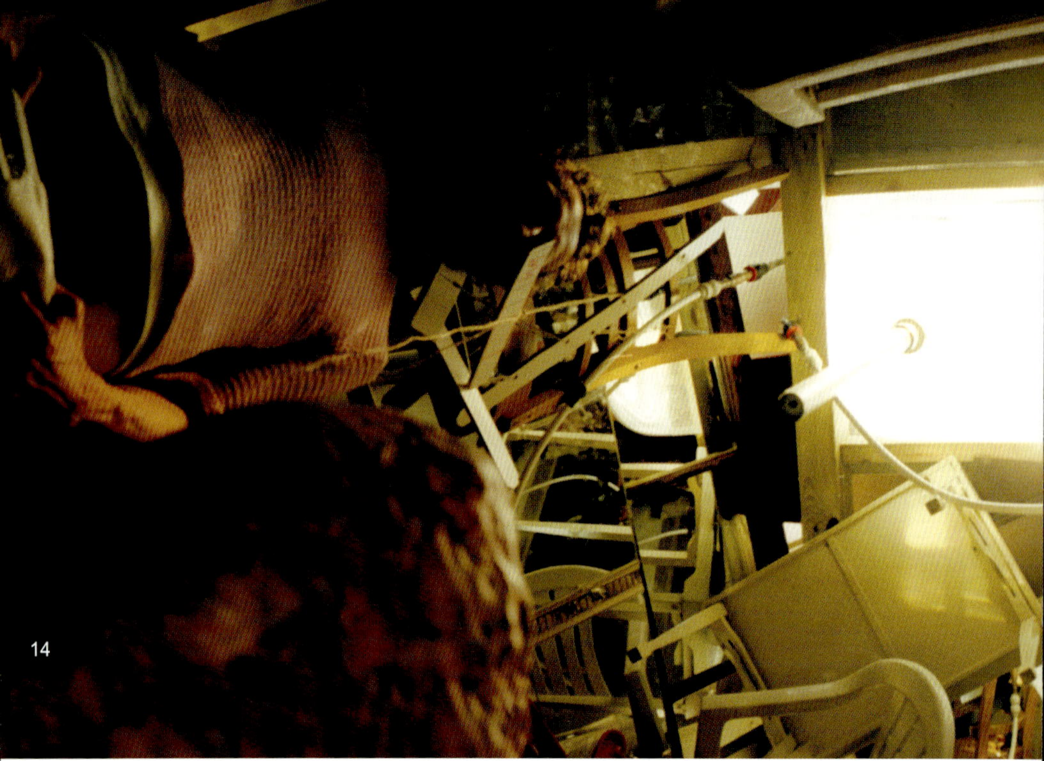

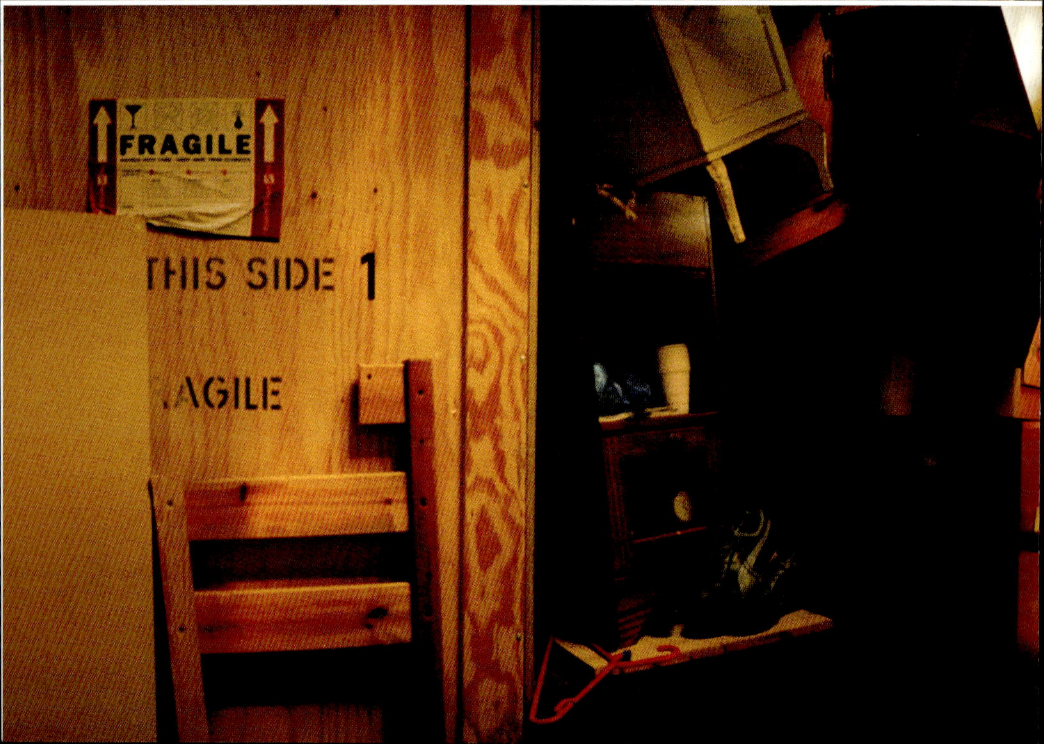

FRAGILE
THIS SIDE 1
AGILE

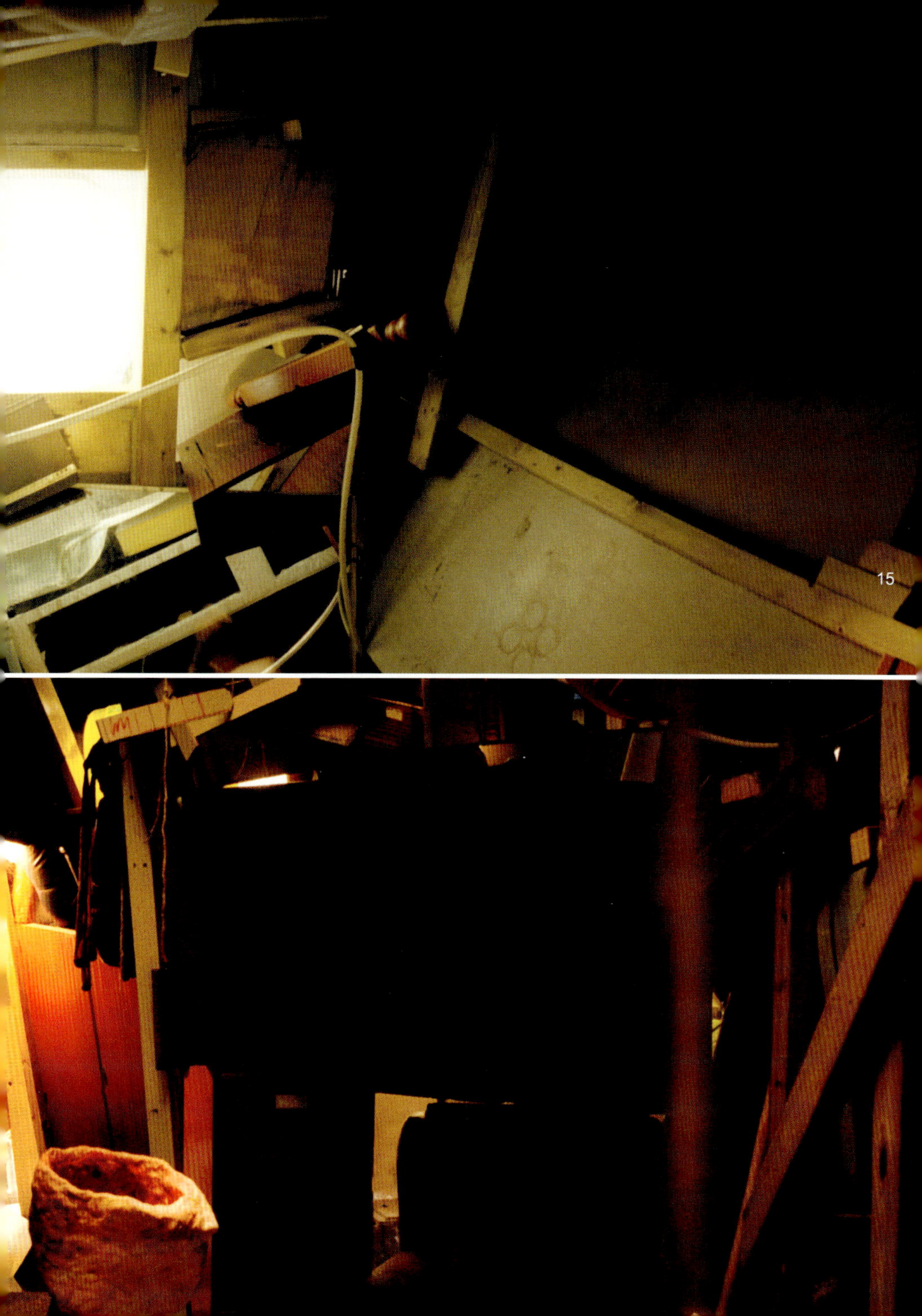

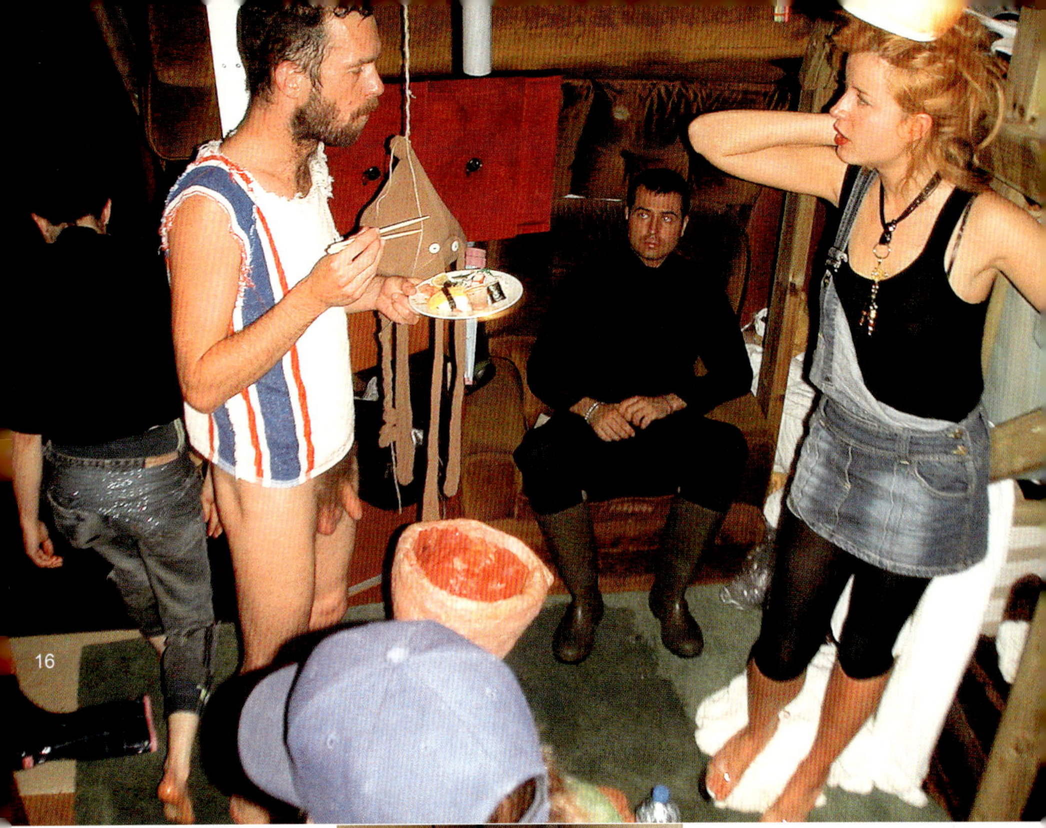

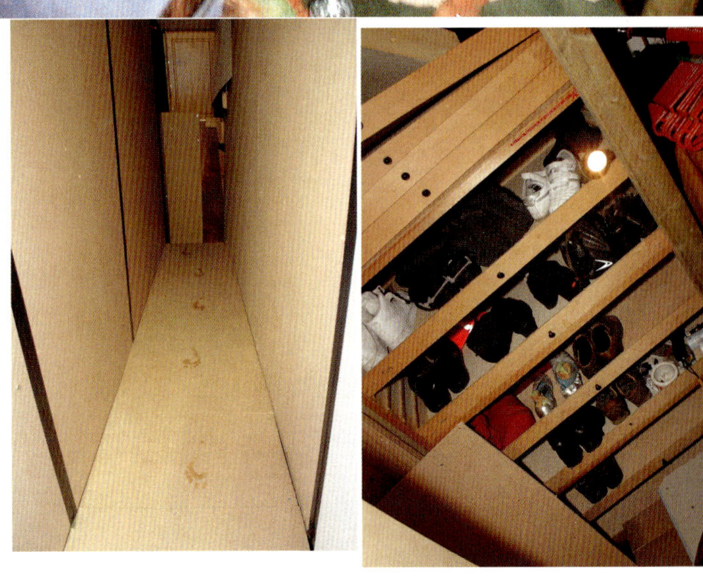

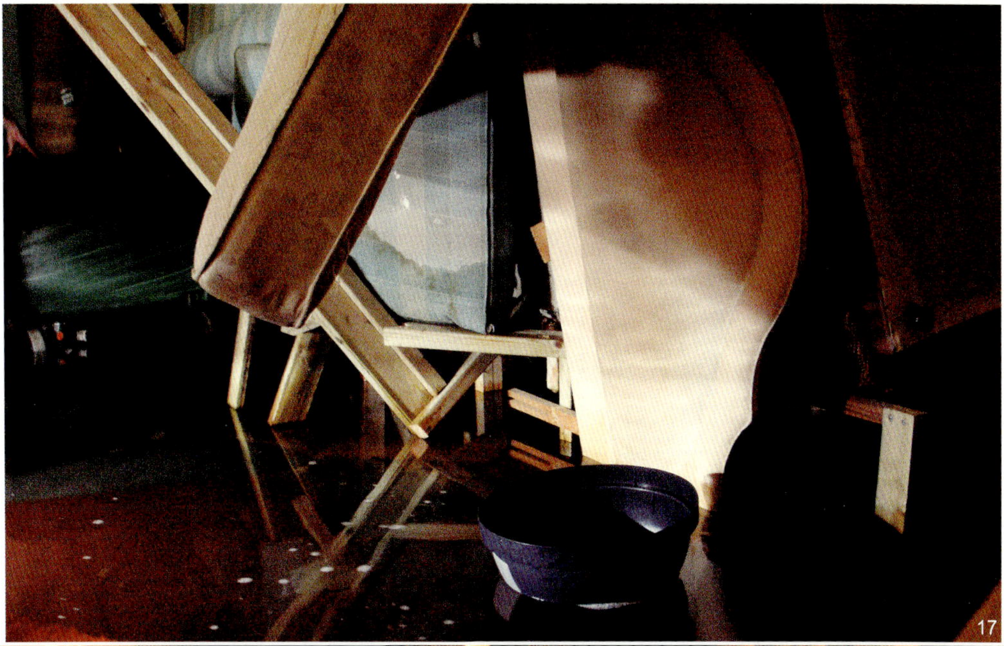

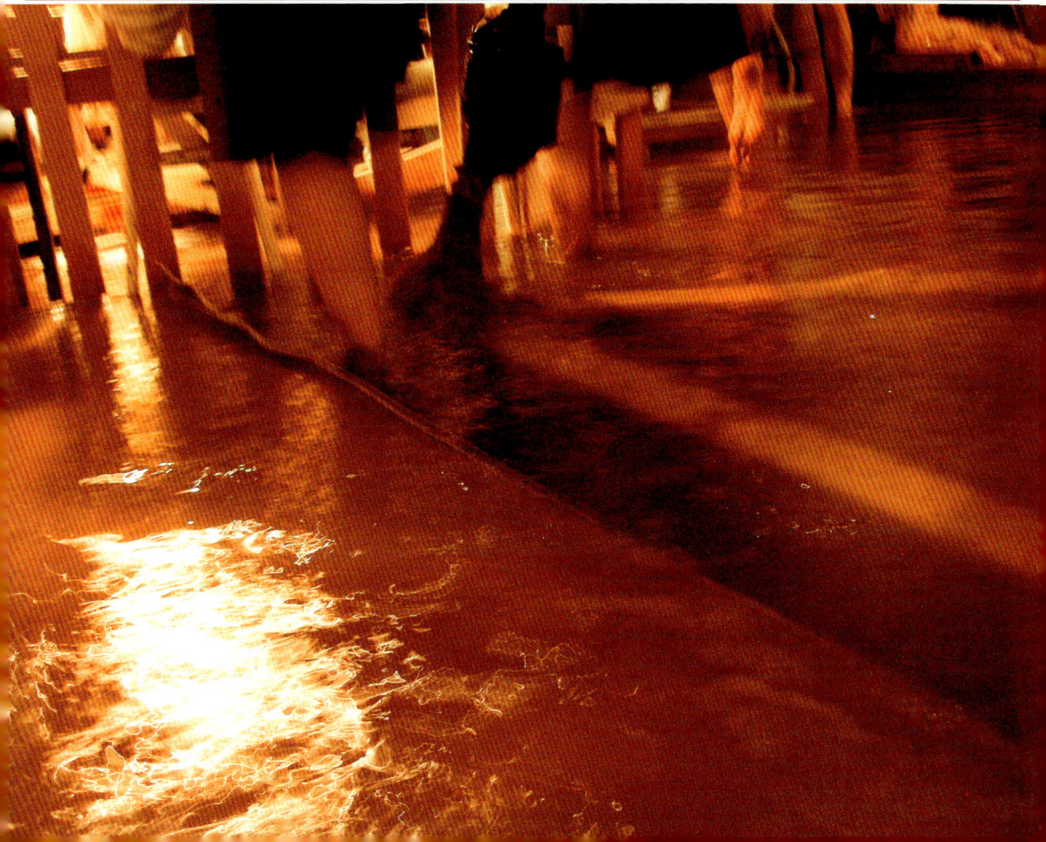

17

18

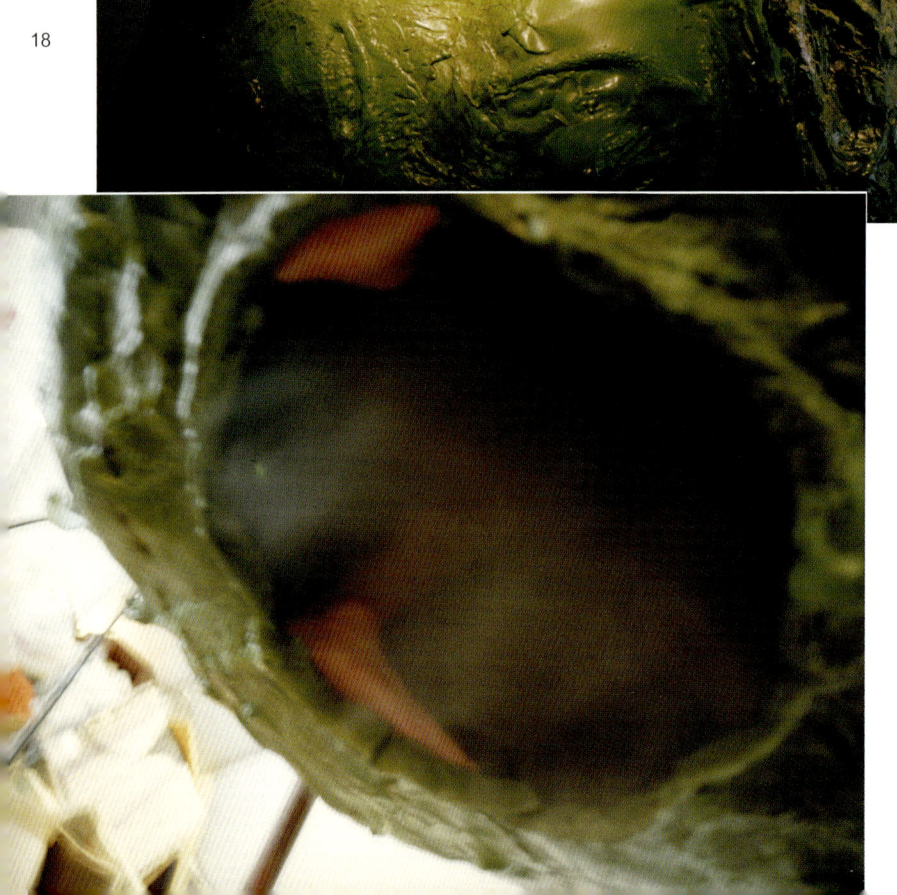

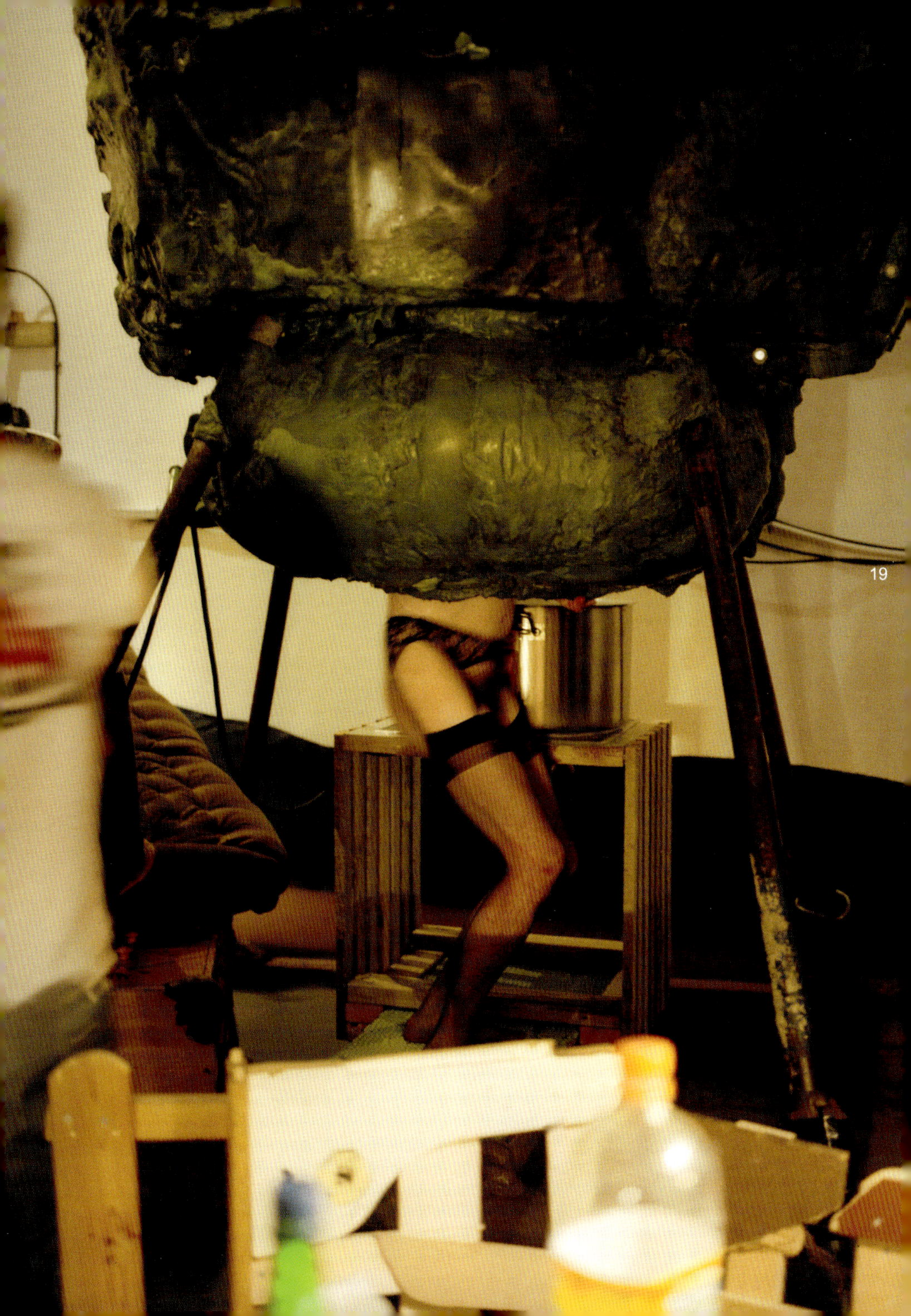
19

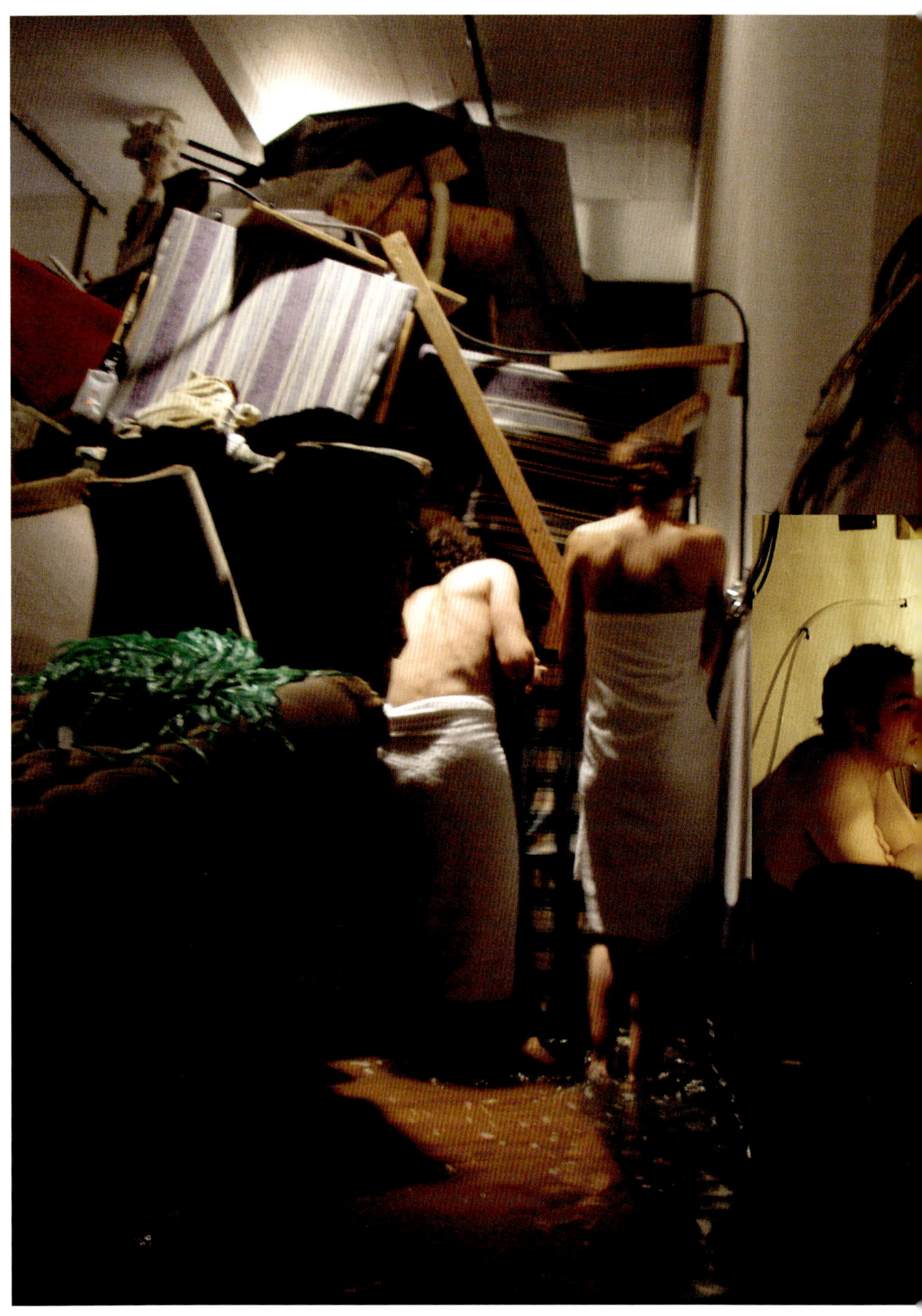

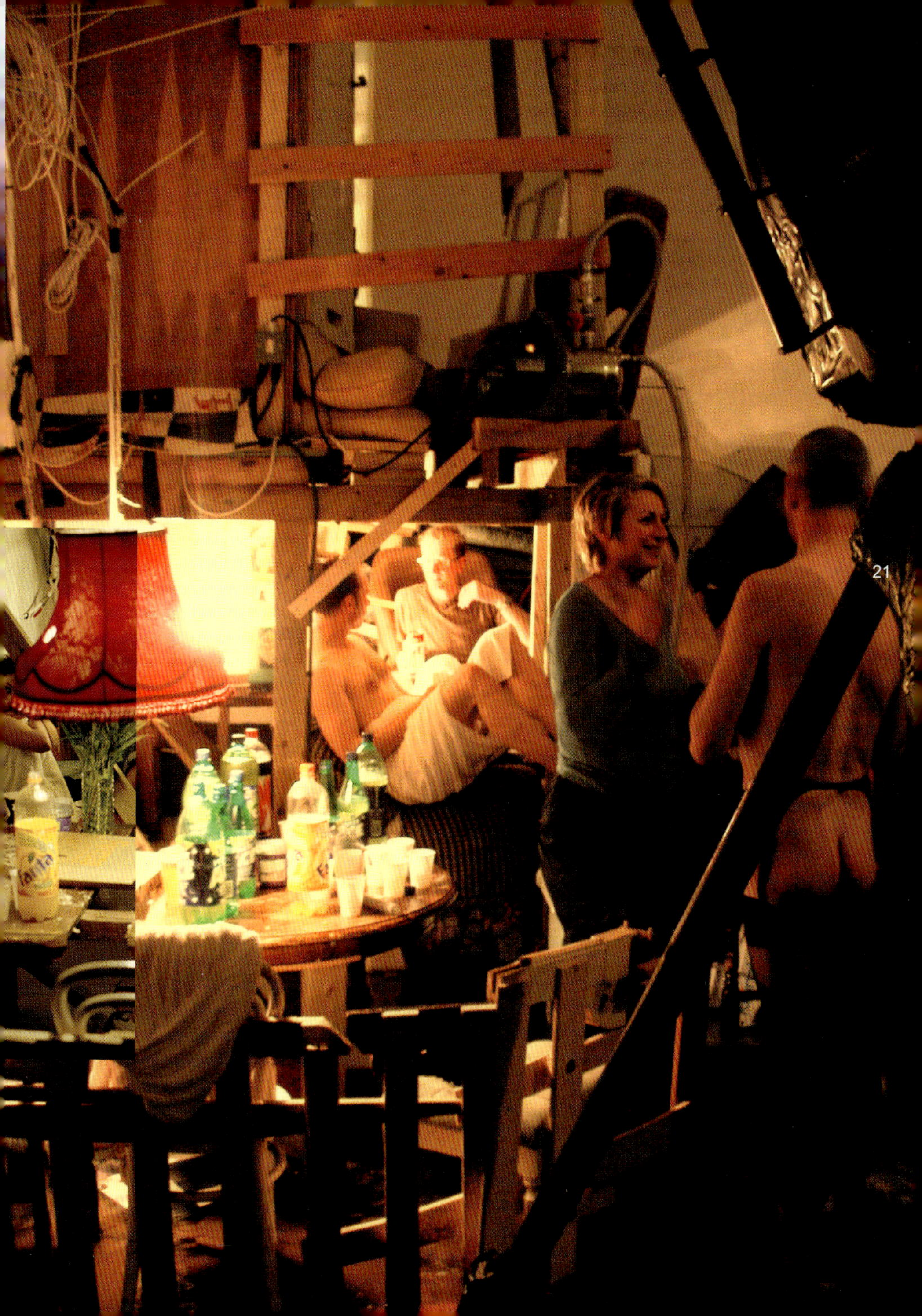

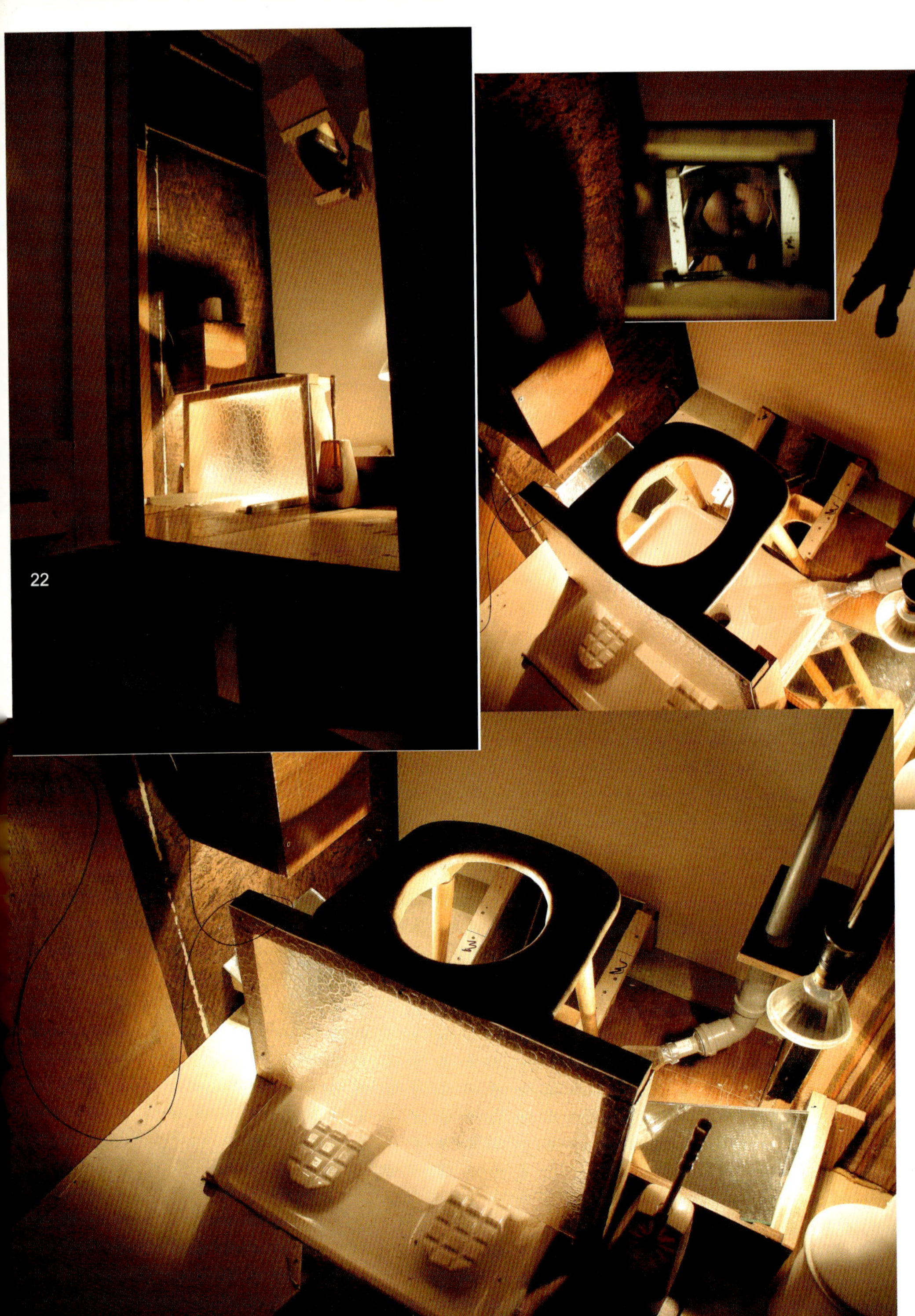

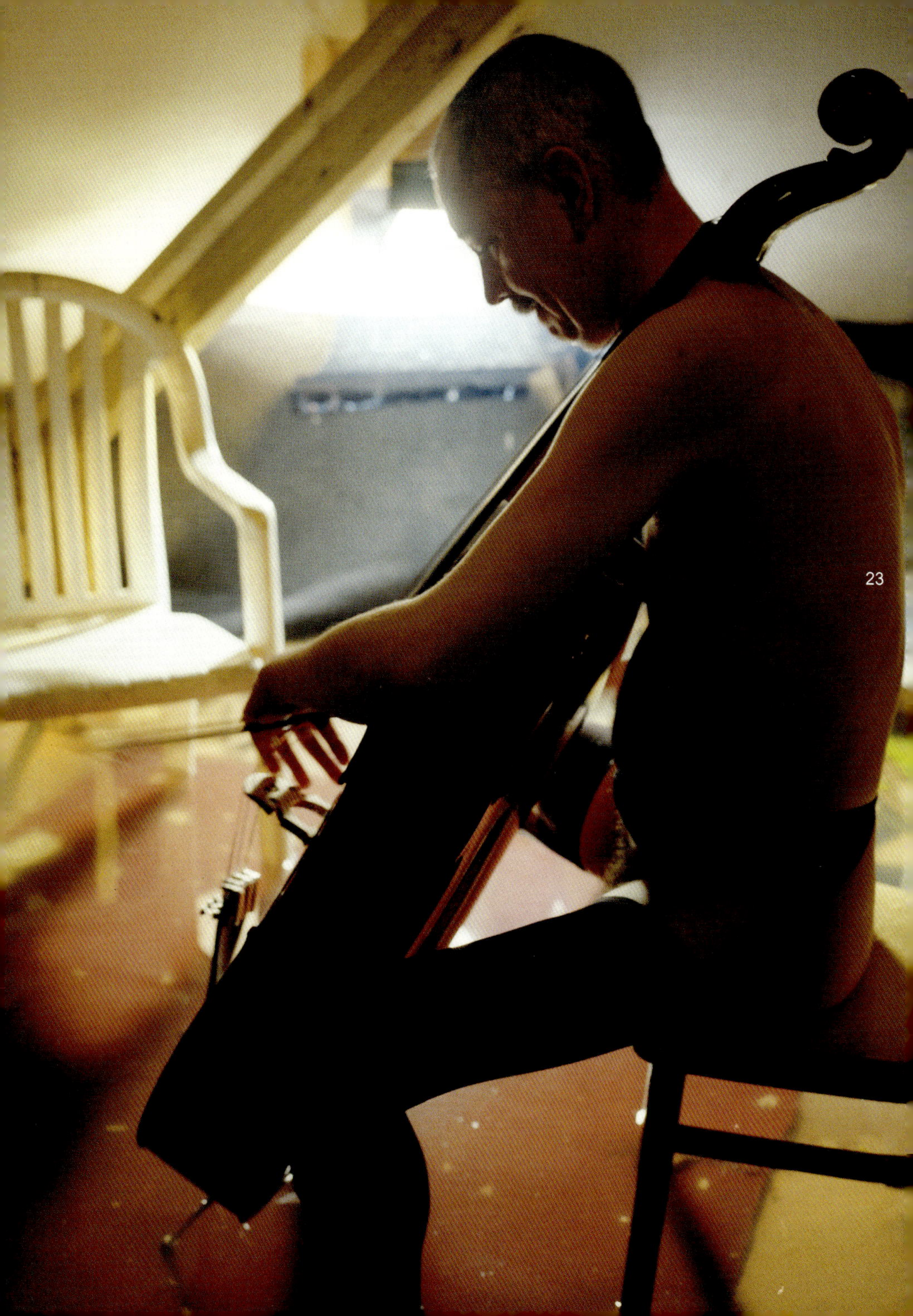

23

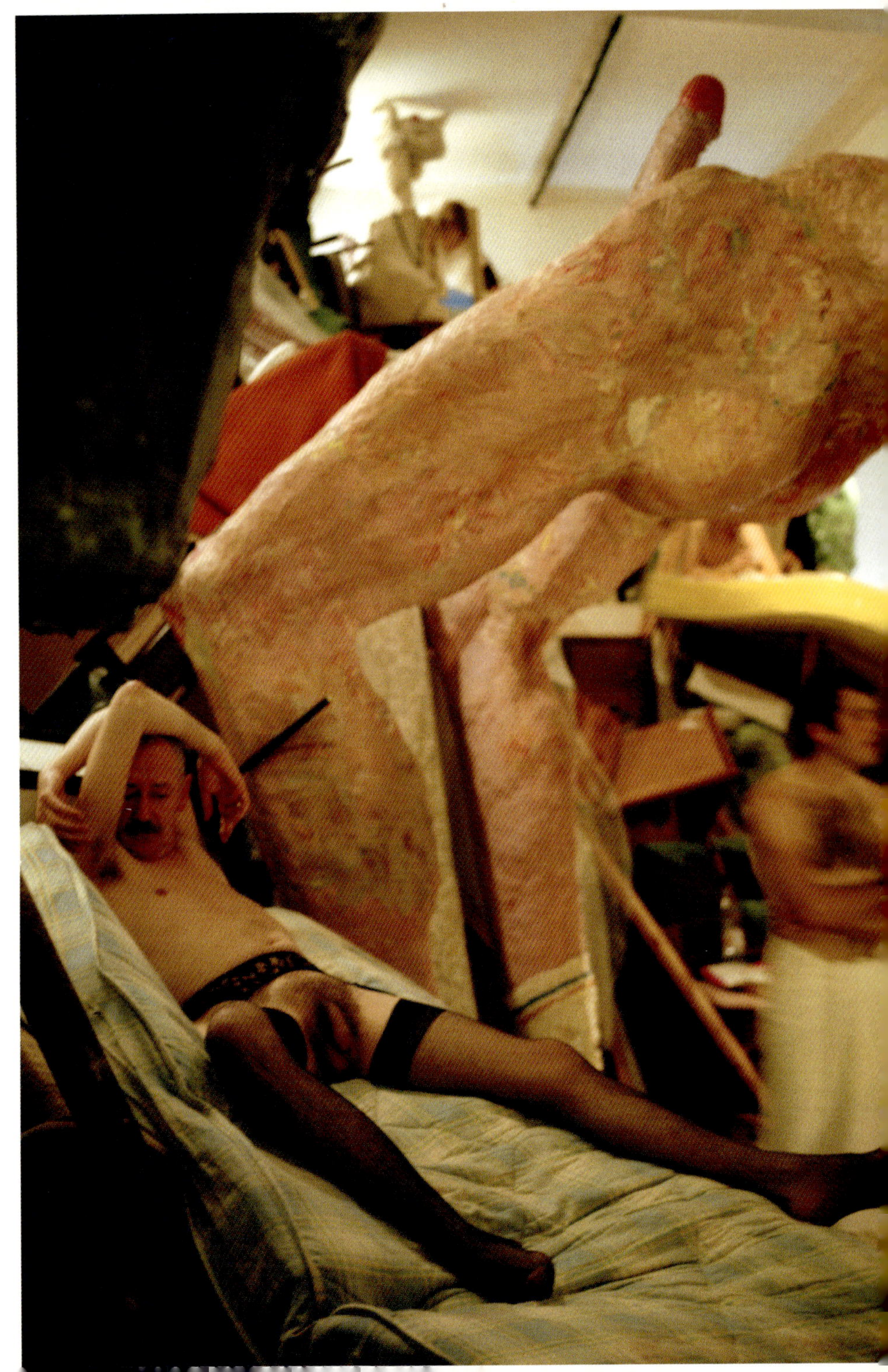

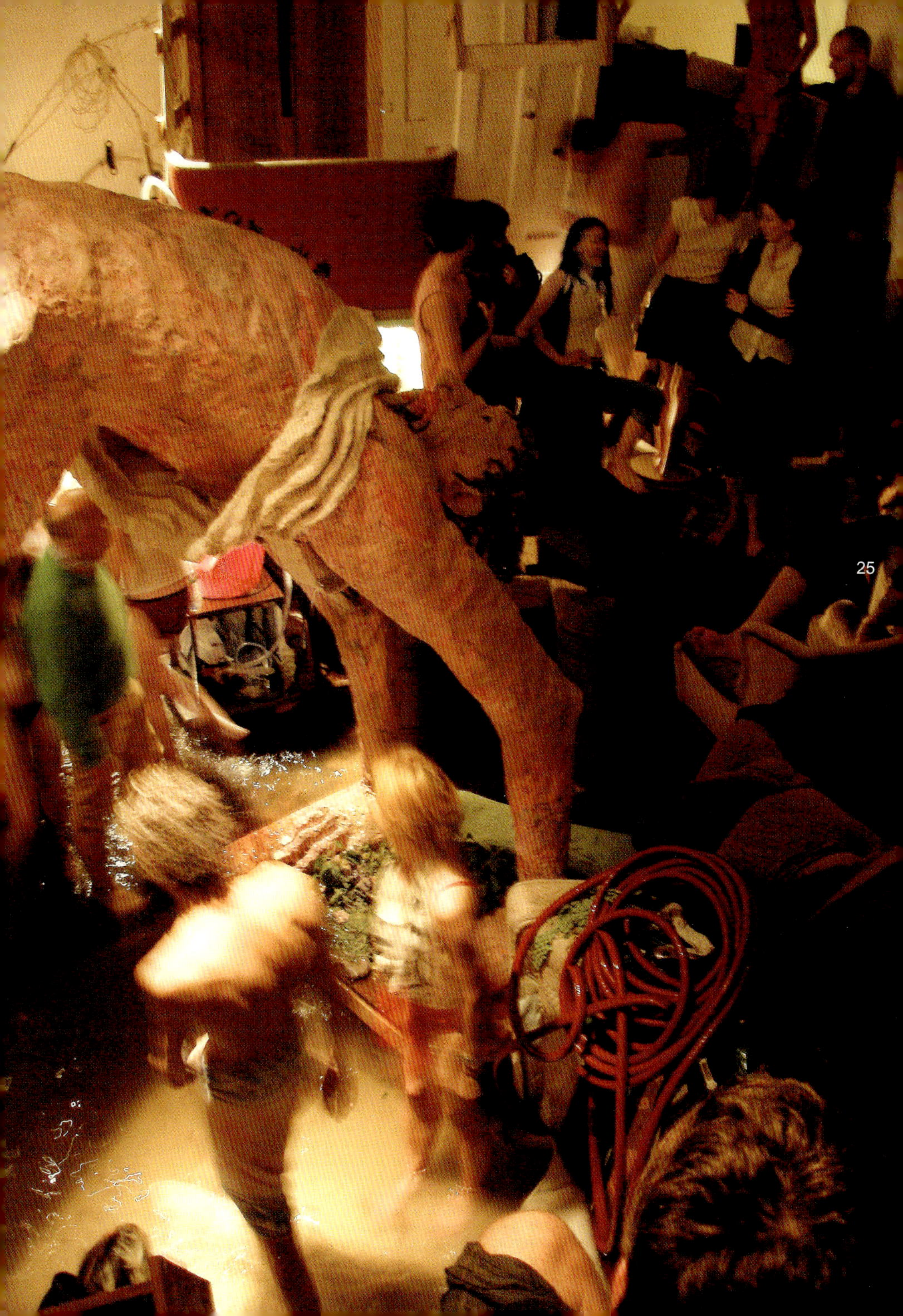

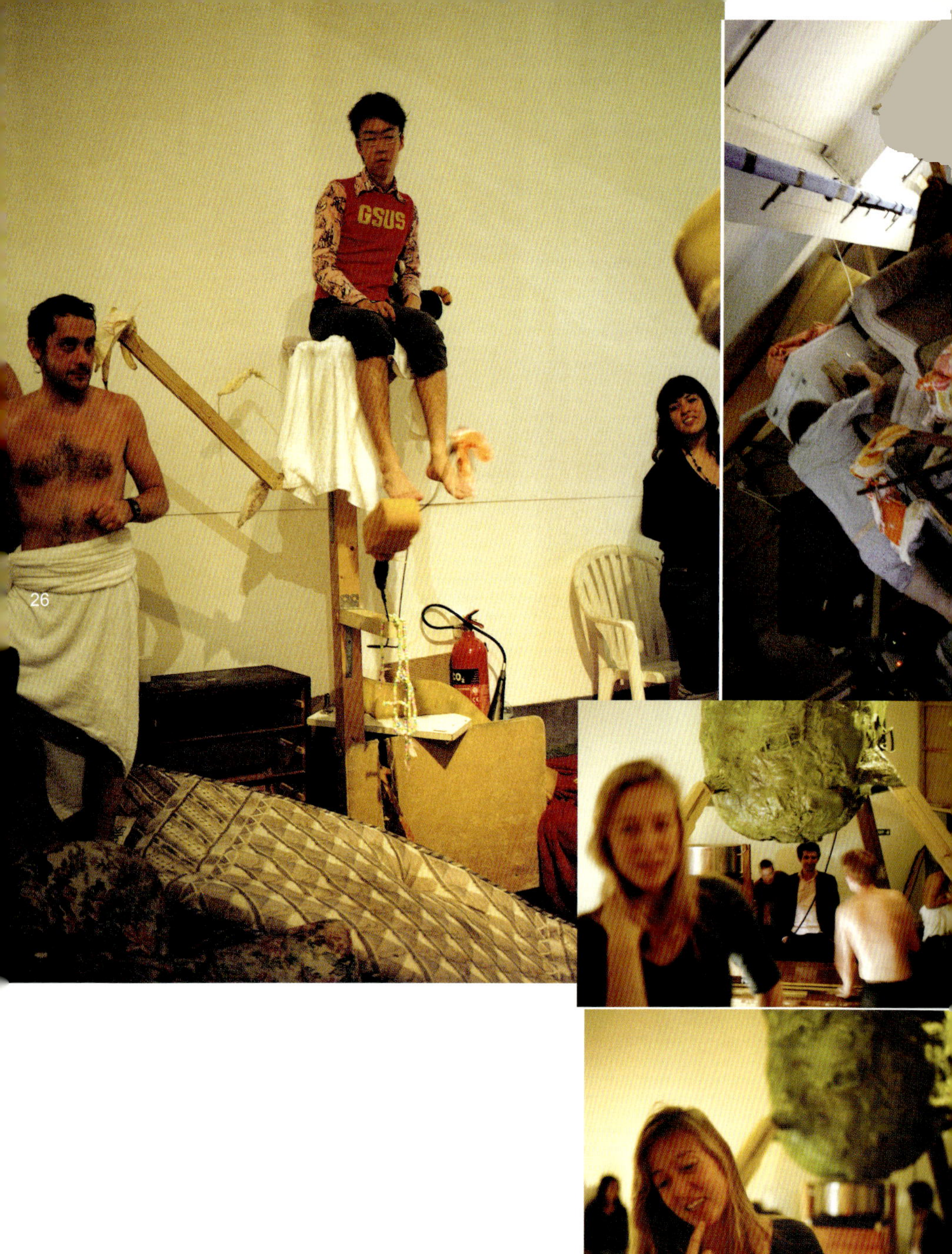

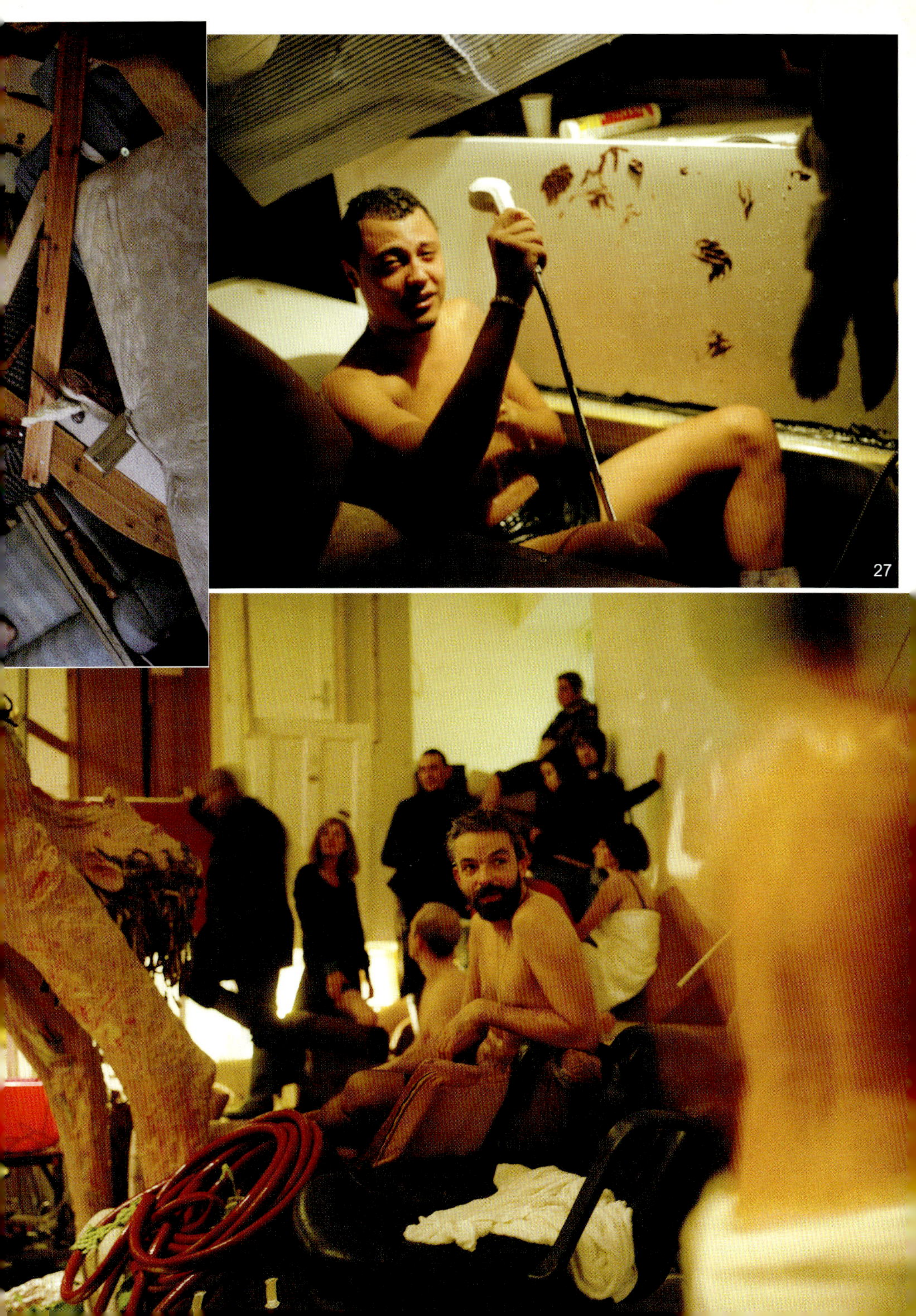

27

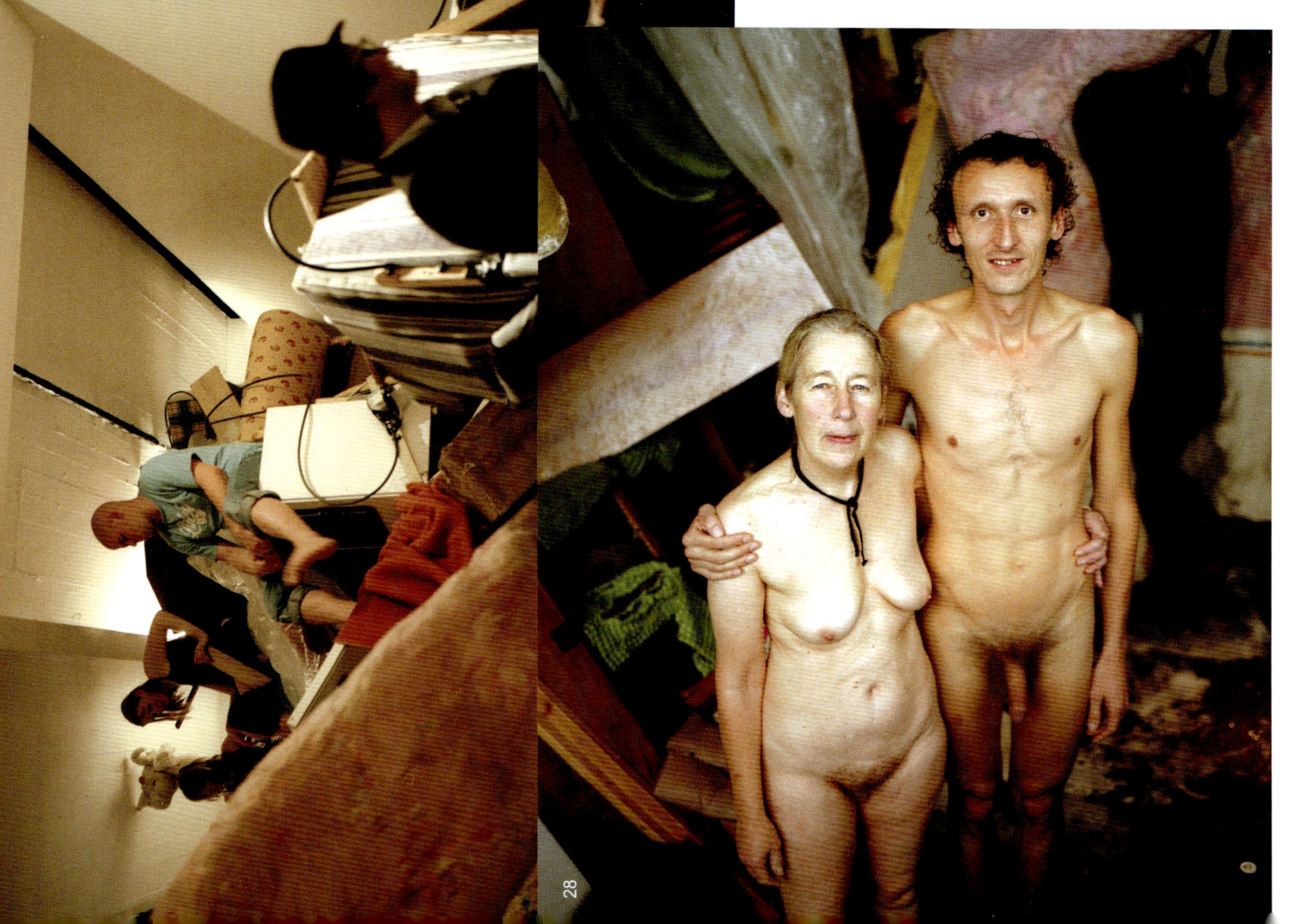

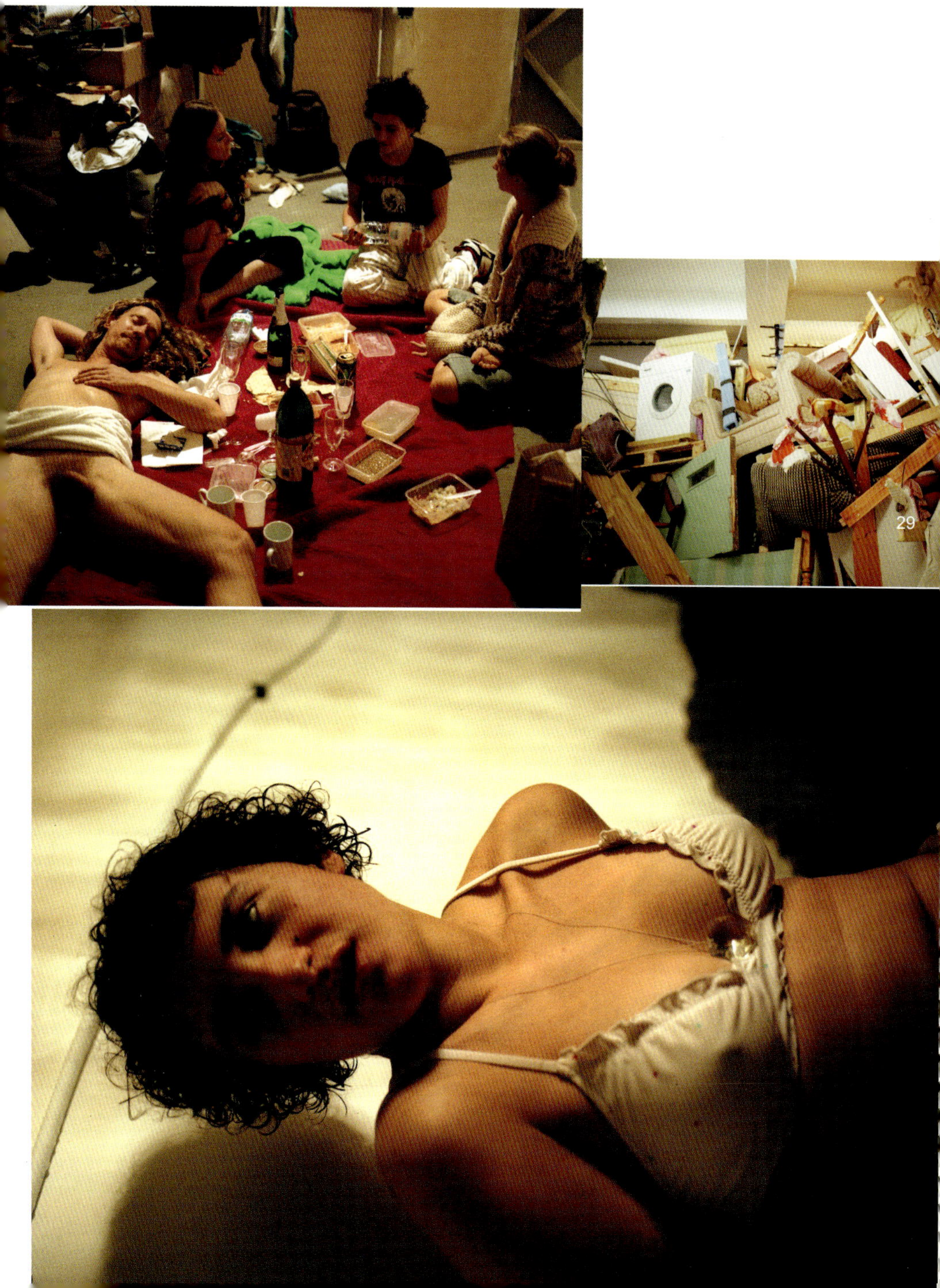

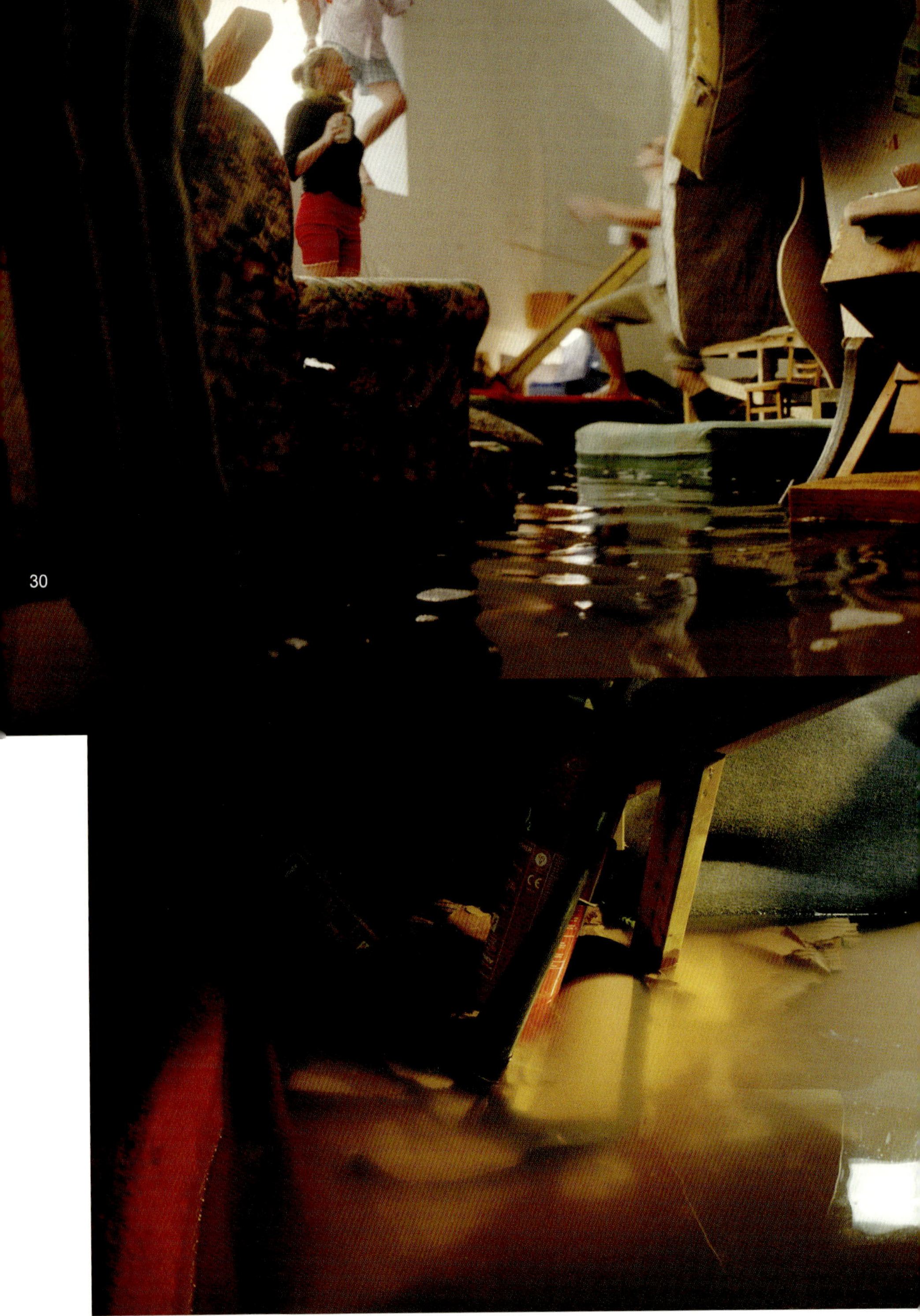

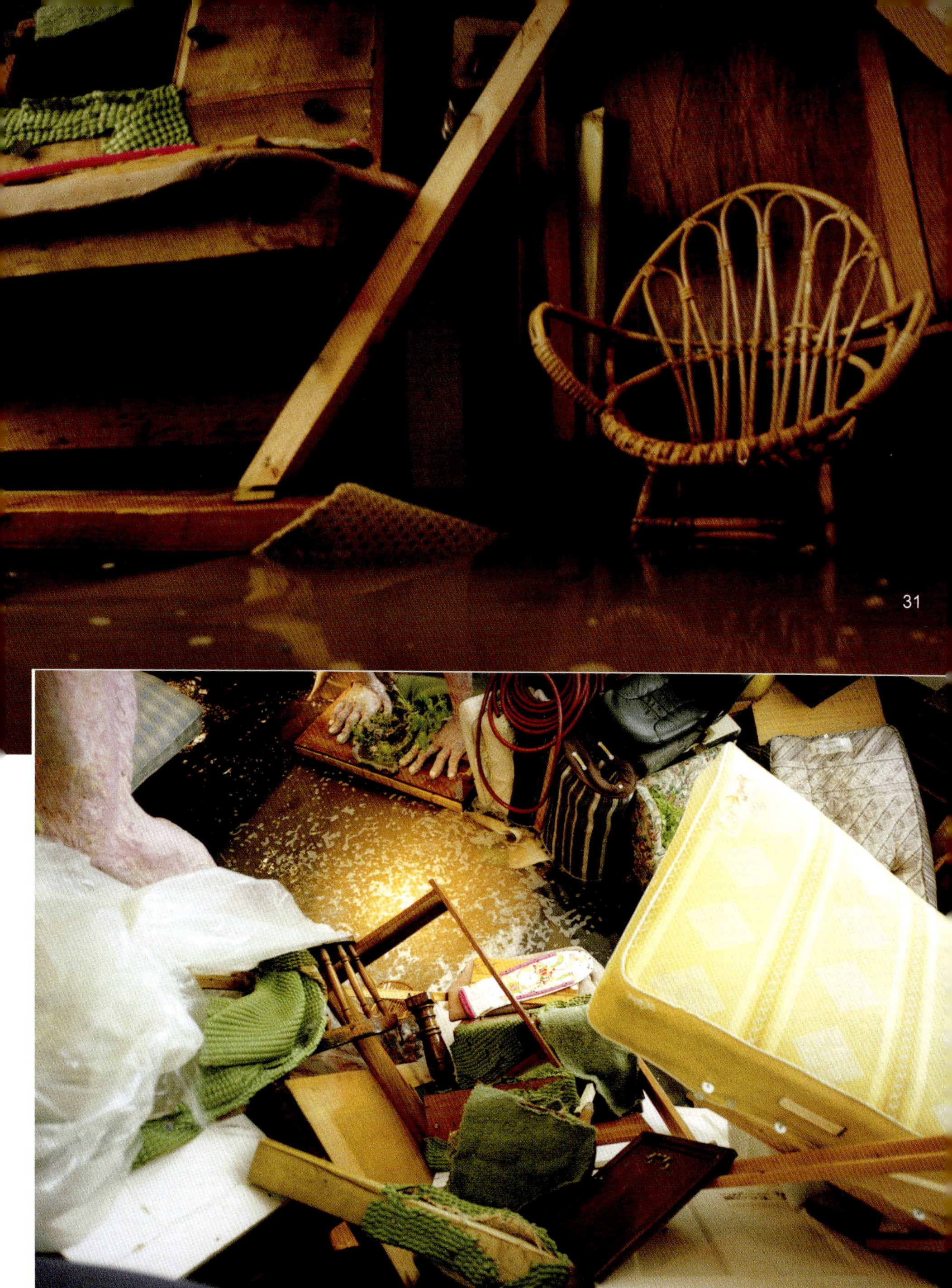

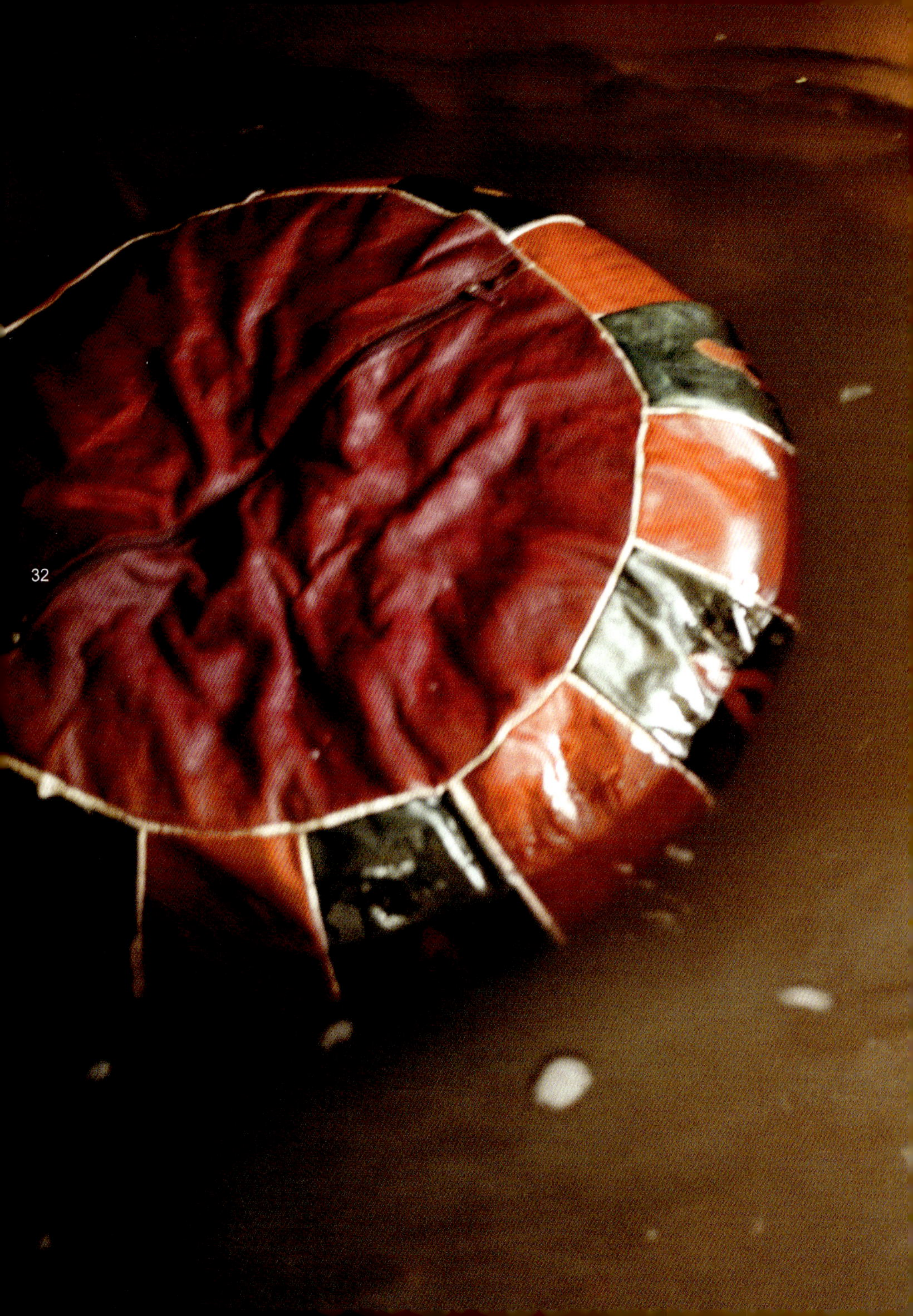

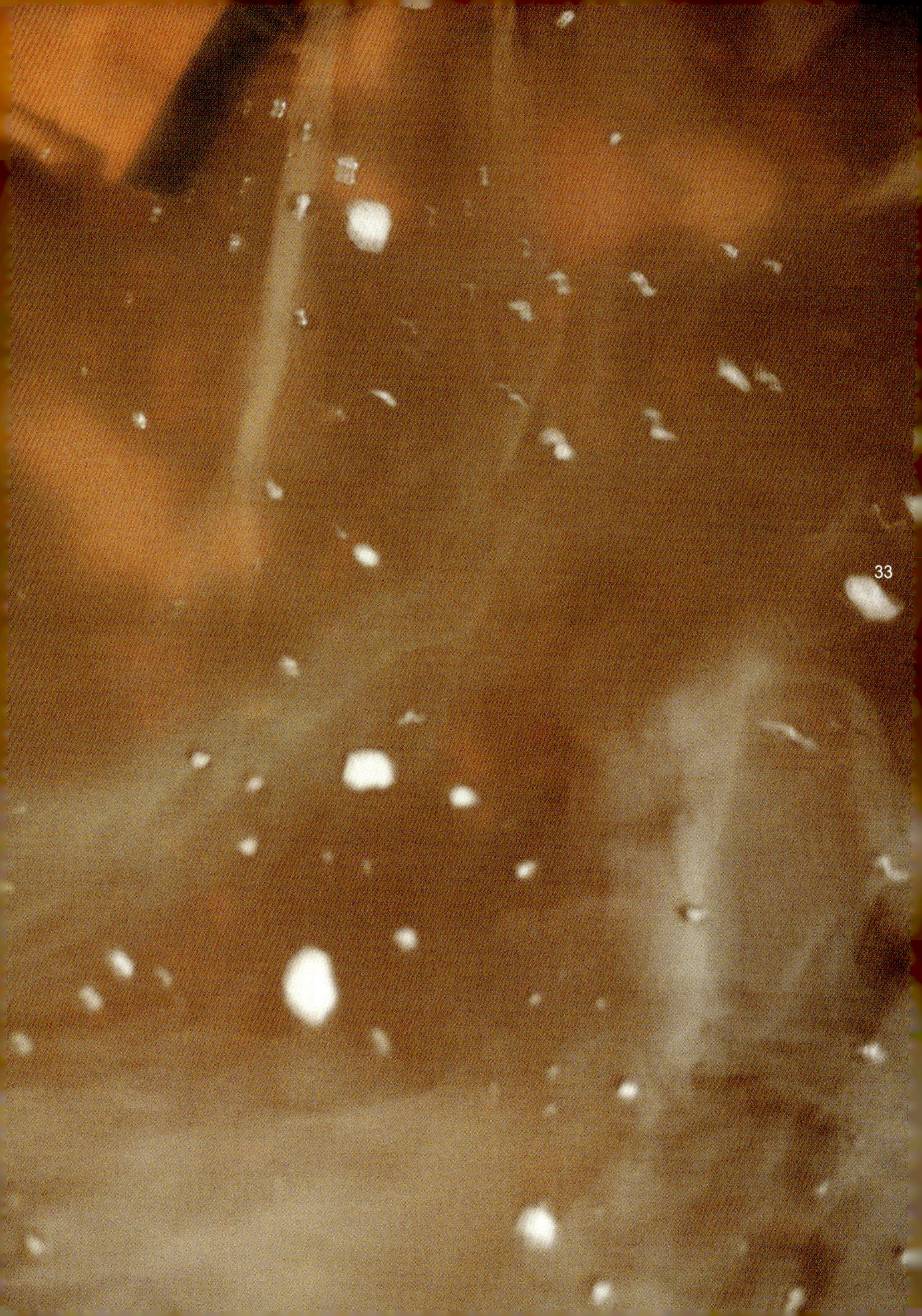

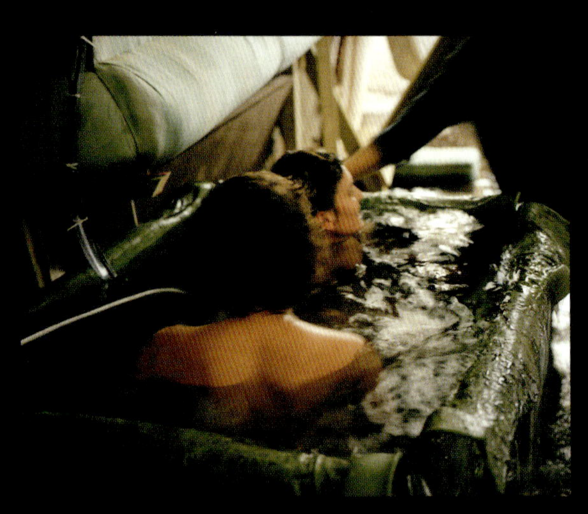

## Puddle Trouble: *Sweatwat* at King's Cross
## by Claire Bishop

Frieze Week 2005: more previews, openings, VIP breakfasts, and knowingly ironic art fair booths than you can shake an empty champagne glass at. Finding myself in King's Cross with a one-hour window between events, I figured it was time to visit the Gelitin boys at Gagosian. After signing a disclaimer at the entrance I climbed up a stepladder, sidled along a thin wooden corridor, and descended to a mirrored changing-room cum chill-out-lounge. Mellow Germanic youths were sprawled around this angular wardrobe area, and encouraged me to exchange my trousers and trainers for a white towel. I'd been expecting some form of disrobing to be necessary, having met one of the Gelitins the previous weekend and asked him what to wear to the event. He had recommended "nudity".

From the dank confines of the changing zone it was a case of splashing through a cold and revoltingly flooded floor (carpets and cardboard bobbed underfoot), past a stack of stained mattresses, to emerge into an open space that resembled a low-budget water garden. The bulk of the room was filled with a ceiling-high mountain of crappy old furniture that supported a splashy waterfall; at its base, a large pink figure of an arch-backed male with a vast erection spouted yet more water onto a pathetic collection of plants. Cerith Wyn Evans moved into view and gestured towards the genital decor. "Here," he announced, full of blissful appreciation, "They have challenged themselves to make the ugliest sculpture in the world. I think they are very close." He poured me a plastic cup of Ice White, a chemical impersonation of cider whose rancid bouquet made the installation's heady dank stink of old furniture seem marginally less oppressive.

Proudly assuming the role of guide, Cerith gestured towards some cubicles in the top left-hand corner of the room. "Up there is the bathroom, a wonderful piece of engineering with see-through pipes." "Does it take solid performances?" One of the gentle Gelitins intercepted before Cerith could answer. Half-naked, his cock nudging through a green plastic Hawaiian skirt, he encouraged me to experience one of their two saunas — a knobbly green homemade pod fuelled by boiling water. As I inserted my head into this fearful sweaty capsule I felt an instant surge of claustrophobic nausea. The idea that you could get seven people in the pod was fascinating and slightly erotic but, on balance, mostly repellent. On the other side of the room, another Gelitin happily removed his underwear (miniscule, but with a long knitted appendage) and leapt inside the other pod. He emerged five minutes later, beatifically gleaming with sweat.

My feet were now freezing in the water, so I retreated to a small and semi-dry platform in the centre of the room. It provided a good outlook onto the toilet and new arrivals to my right, a sauna pod to my left and the furniture mountain ahead. There was a quiet tinkling of water and occasional activity as various Gelitins and their visitors intermittently descended from the green pods, socialised in the kitchen, or scrambled up and down the stack of chairs and mattresses. When the waterfall stopped flowing, I figured it was time to mount the damp and grubby sofa stack and see what was up there. Clambering over the stained furniture I found a pool, a see-through bathtub offering a distorted vista down onto the chill-out changing room below. The water was unappealingly tepid. Beyond the pool there was a warm room brimming with yet more rancid soft furnishings, inhabited by two chunky female visitors who clearly had installed themselves there for some time. After a few minutes I left, intimidated, and began the long haul back to the water garden. Beatrix Ruf became visible as I descended — majestic in full curatorial black, and looking totally out of place. Standing next to her was Cerith, who had now changed into his performance gear — wellies and a resplendent pair of Y-fronts emblazoned with the tackle of Michelangelo's *David*. I was tempted to stay on for his performance (a Fluxus-style event involving a cello) but feared the onset of pneumonia and figured it was time to quit. Splish, splish, splash, back to my warm socks.

In retrospect, *Sweatwat* was definitely one of the highlights of Frieze Week — although at the time it was hard to perceive it as more or less substantial than the rest of the too hastily con-sumed art on offer. You have to admire Gelitin's ability to turn the slickest of commercial galleries into an abominably abject playground, flood it with water, and then encourage everyone to prance around it in half-naked. Clearly *Sweatwat* fits into a lineage of ambitious installation experiences using found junk — from Kaprow and Oldenburg in the early '60s to Paul Thek and many others since.  The last five years have seen a revival of this activity in various forms: from the carefully staged room sequences of Mike Nelson to the eccentric chaos of John Bock and the creepy domesticity of Gregor Schneider, whose *Dead House Ur* is probably the closest parallel to *Sweatwat* for sheer grubbiness and olfactory assault. But Gelitin seems less interested in psychologically charged spaces than in pressuring a social dynamic. *Sweatwat* was a space to be used rather than admired, a backdrop to group activity. In this orientation towards the social, the alternative community of *Sweatwat* evokes AVL-Ville, but minus van Lieshout's commitment to good design. It's telling, however, that all my analogies are boy artists. In this panorama of masculine construction work, Gelitin stand out for their playful sexuality. *Sweatwat* was most convincing as a social ecosystem that encouraged, seduced, and (if necessary) coerced you into accepting its own contract of group behaviour. As the hours progressed and the Ice White flowed, people cavorted naked through puddles and thrust themselves in and out of sauna pod love-ins with a carefree spirit I couldn't quite muster at 8pm. In this narrative of flirtation, compression and liberation, *Sweatwat* is archived in my sen-sorium — or should I say, revoltingly vaulted.

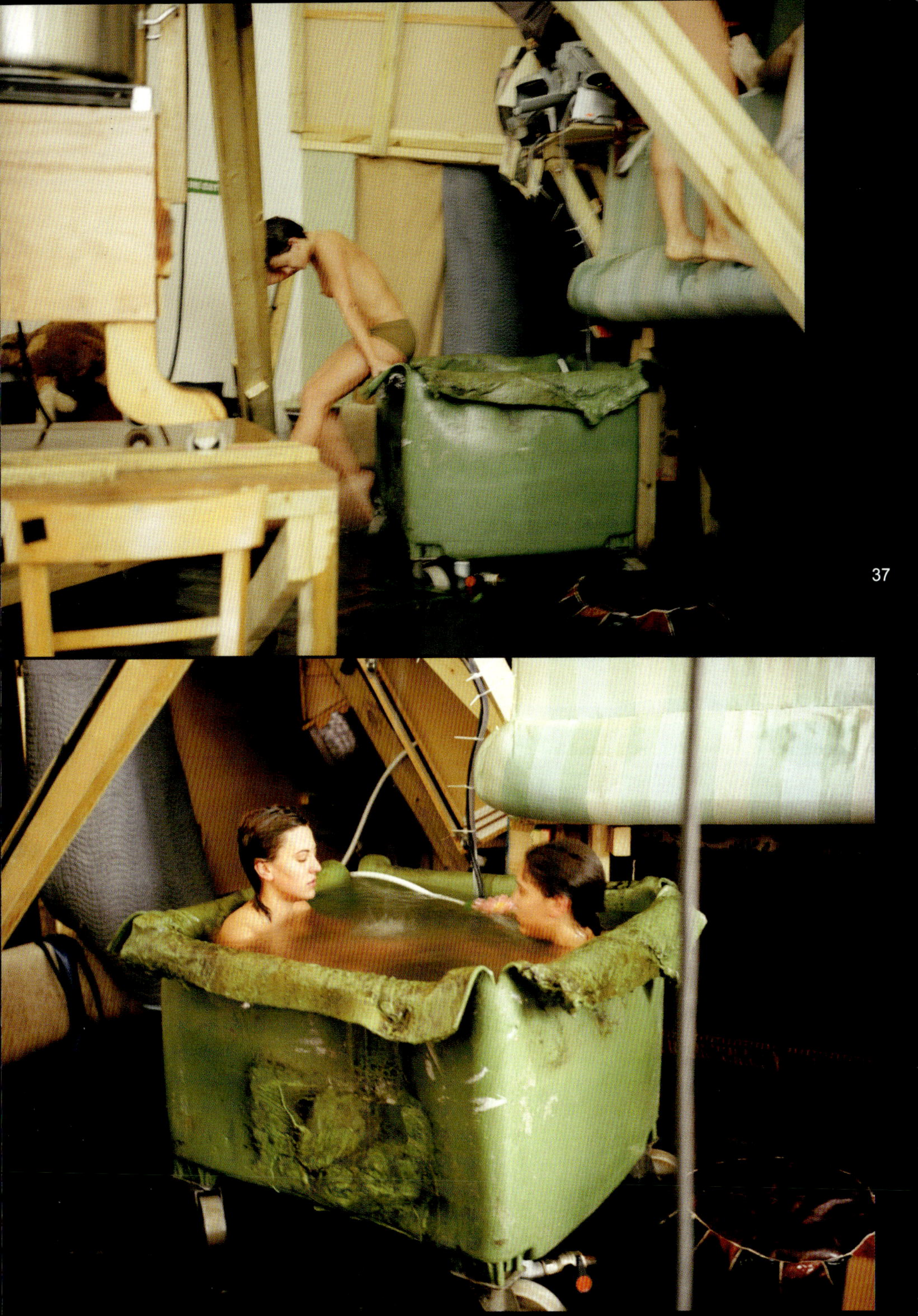

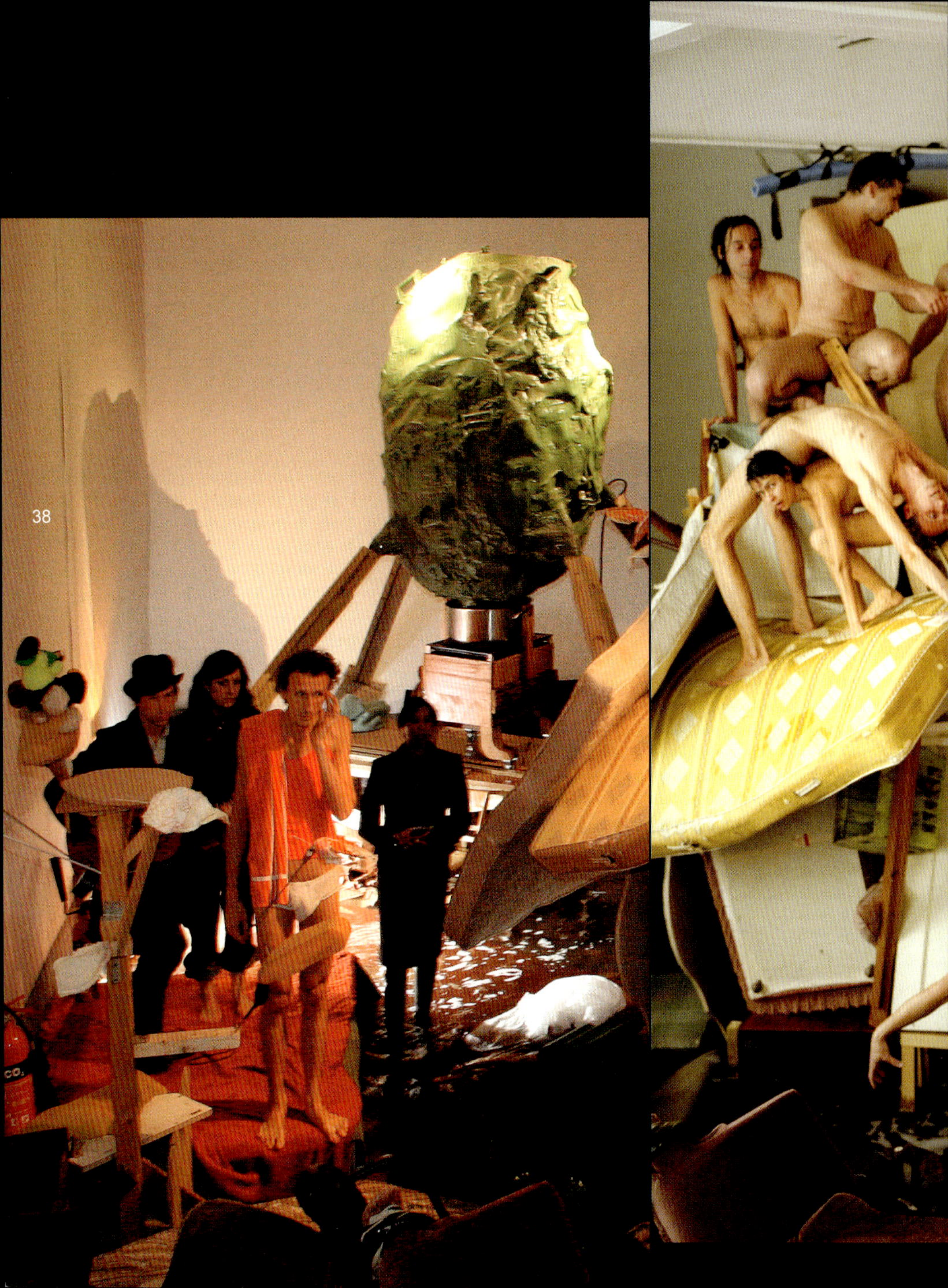

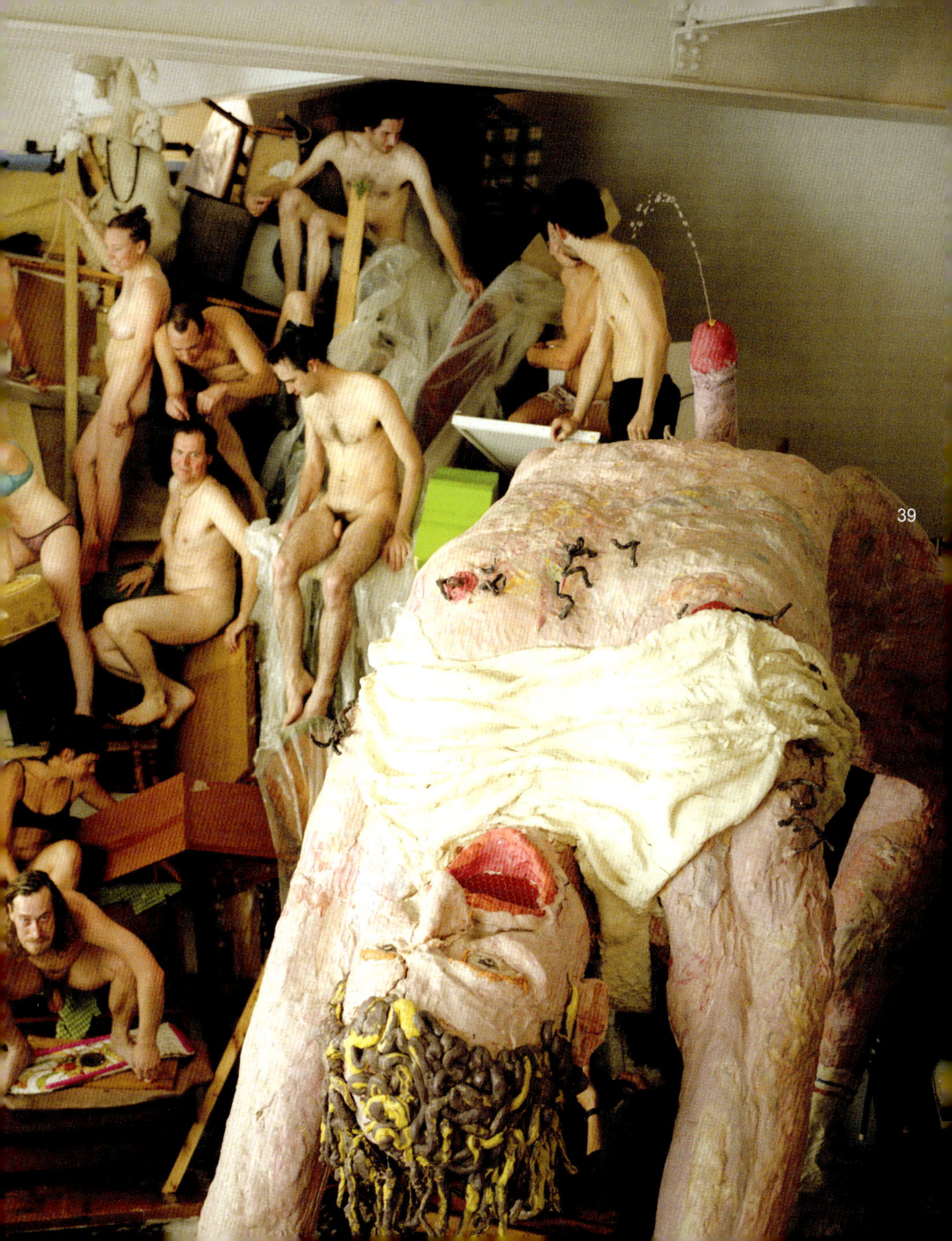

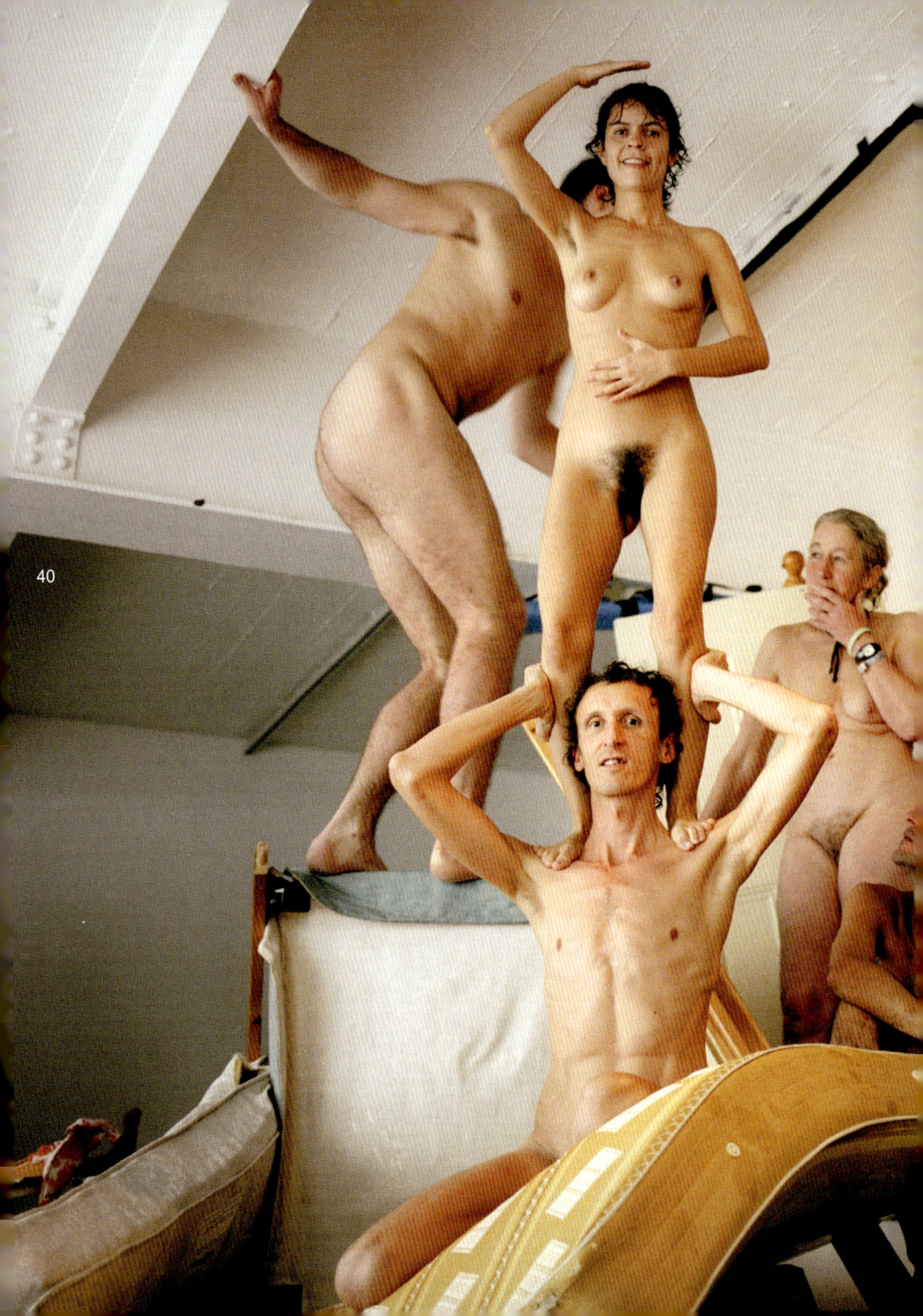

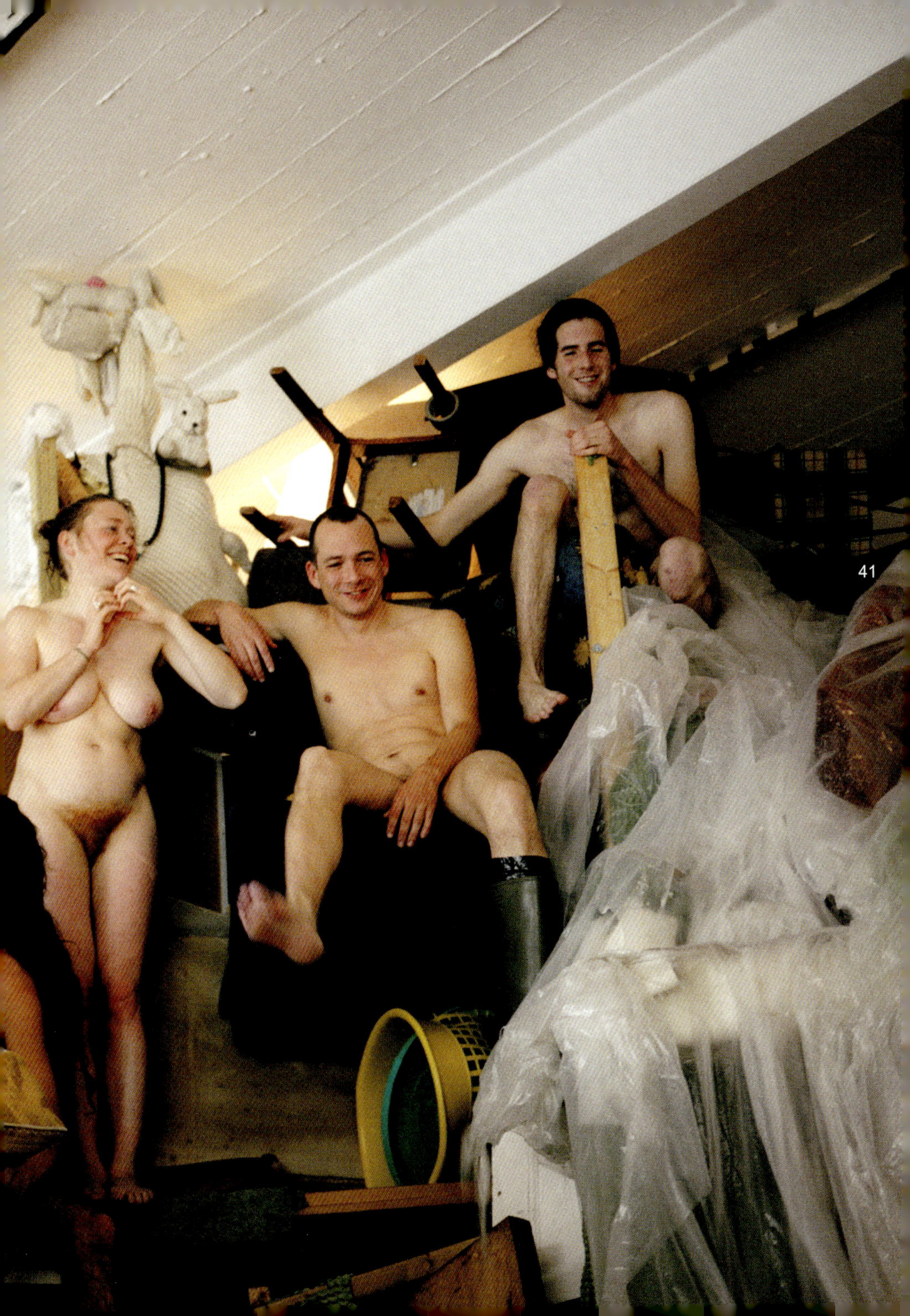

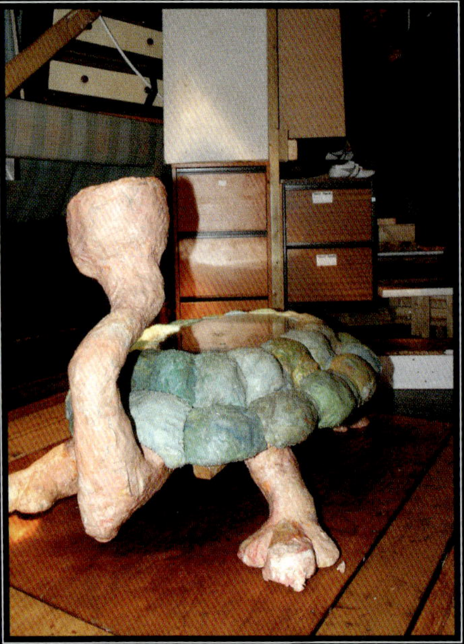

*Rialto*, 2004
Acrylic bathtub, plasticine on wood with mirror and drain.
43 1/4 x 31 1/2 x 27 1/2 inches
(110 x 80 x 70 cm)

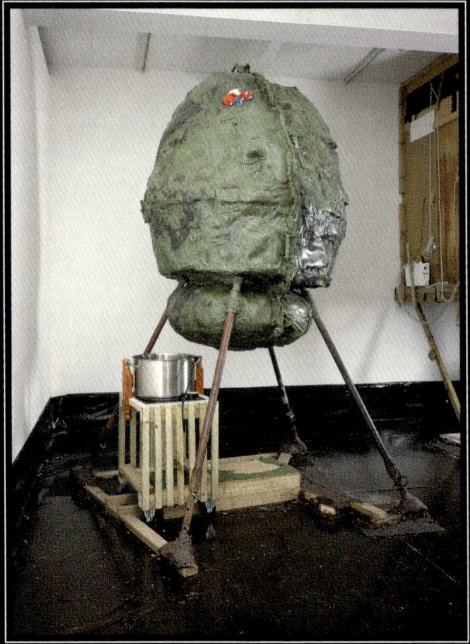

*When I was a Borg I was responsible for the death
of countless millions and I didn't feel anything*, 2005
Sauna for six people: melted plastic rubbish bins, wooden
platform with electric hob and large pan.
Dimensions variable

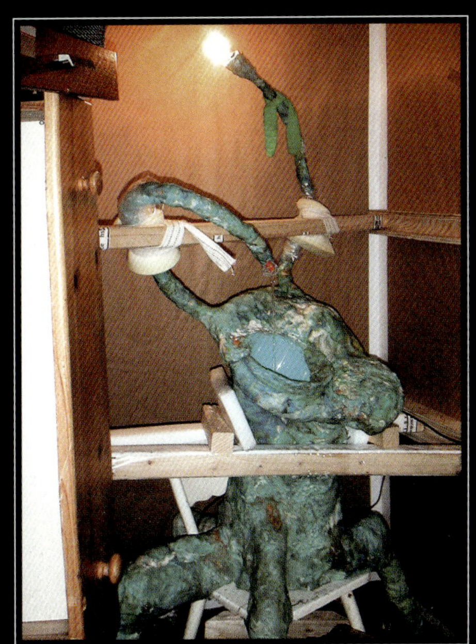



*In the eye lingers the taste of another man,* 2005
Plasticine, plastic and wood with drain.
27 1/2 x 27 1/2 x 78 3/4 inches
(70 x 70 x 200 cm)

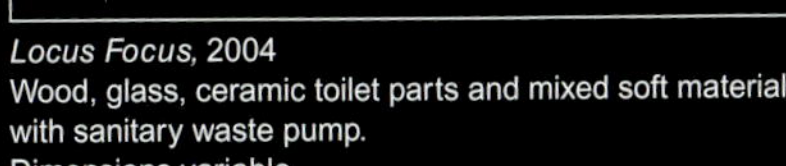

*Locus Focus,* 2004
Wood, glass, ceramic toilet parts and mixed soft materials
with sanitary waste pump.
Dimensions variable

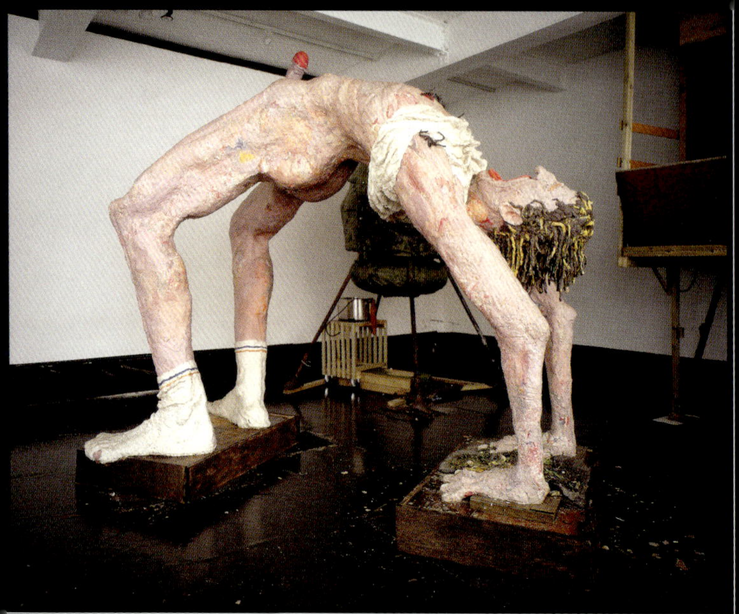

*Arc de Triomphe,* 2003
Plasticine on wood and metal, with fountain pump.
78 3/4 x 118 x 118 inches
(200 x 300 x 300 cm)

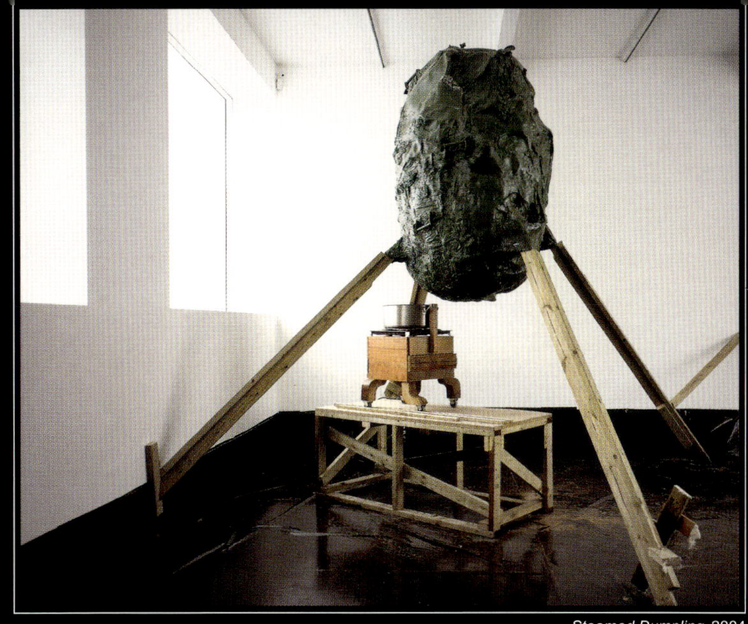

*Steamed Dumpling*, 2004
Sauna for three people: melted plastic rubbish bins, wooden
platform with electric hob and large pan. Plus cold water
plastic container bath with ice machine.
Dimensions variable

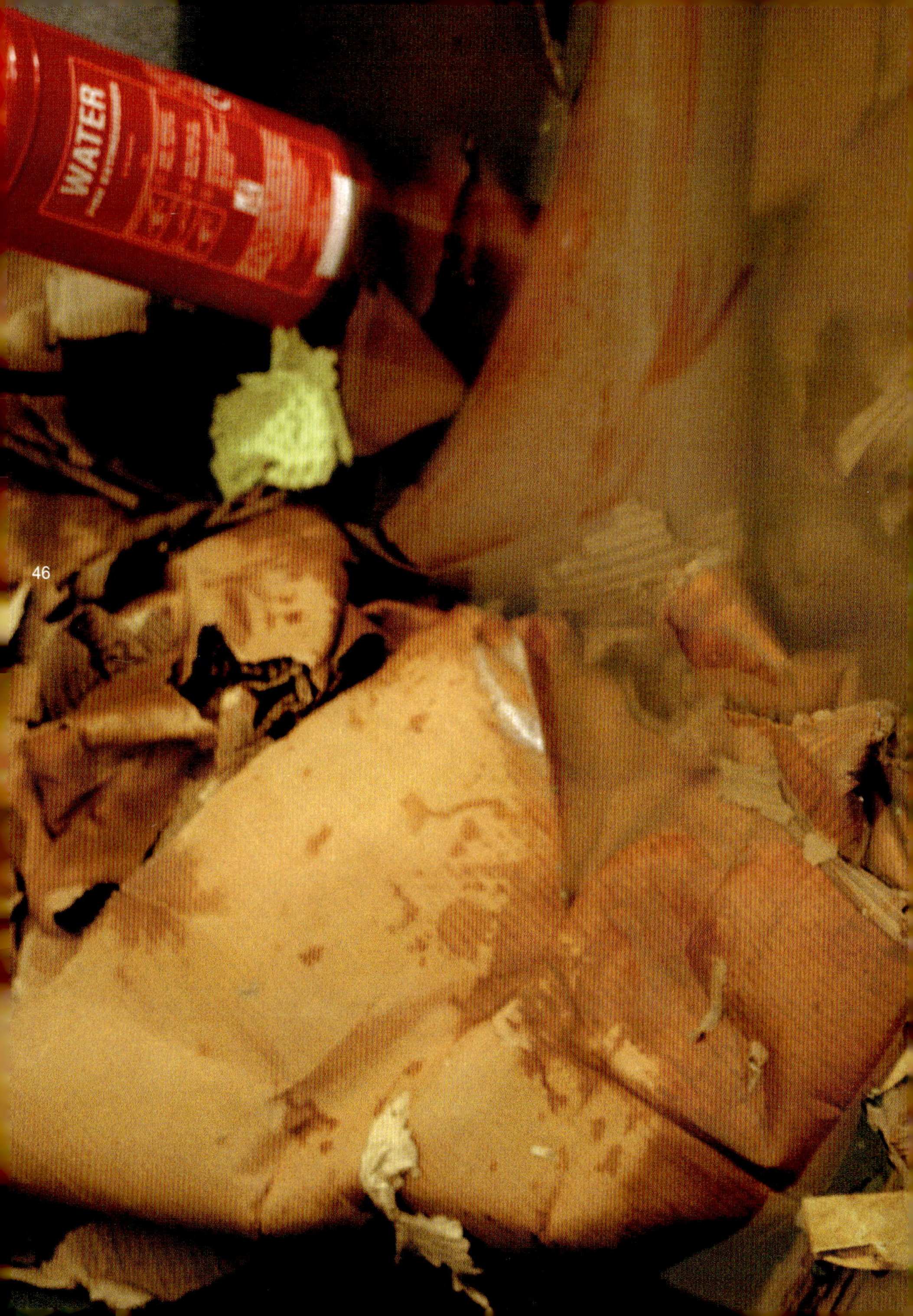
WATER

**2005**

*Tantamounter 24/7, PERFORMA05,* Performance
  Biennale, Leo Koenig Inc., New York
*Sweatwat,* Gagosian Gallery, London
*Hase,* Permanent Installation, Artesina, Italy
*Les Grands Spectacles,* Museum der Moderne,
  Salzburg, Austria
*X Wohnungen,* Märkisches Viertel, Hebbel am Ufer,
  Berlin
*Bilder hauen — Skulpturen bauen,* Zoom
  Kindermuseum Museumsquartier, Vienna, Austria
*Les innocents aux pieds sales,* Performance,
  Galerie Emmanuel Perrotin, Paris
*Dionysiac,* Centre Georges Pompidou, Paris
*Zapf de Pipi,* Moscow Biennale, Moscow

**2004**

*Nasser Klumpatsch,* Institute of Contemporary
  Art Sofia, Sofia, Bulgaria
*Möbelsalon Käsekrainer,* Galerie Meyer Kainer,
  Vienna, Austria
*Otto Volante,* Galleria Massimo De Carlo, Milan, Italy

**2003**

*Gelatin at the Shore of Lake Pippi Kacka,*
  Performance, Frieze Art Fair, London
*The Gelatin Institut,* Leo Koenig Inc., New York
*Dessinez avec Desiree,* Galerie Meyer Kainer,
  Vienna, Austria
*Im Arsch des Elefanten steckt ein Diamant,*
  Schirn Kunsthalle, Siemens Arts Program,
  Frankfurt, Germany
*Arc de Triomphe,* Rupertinum Salzburg, Austria
*Golden Shower,* Performance, Schirn Kunsthalle,
  Frankfurt, Germany

**2002**

*Win Win,* Shanghai Biennale, Shanghai, China
*Le Cadeau,* Galerie Emmanuel Perrotin, Paris
*Die Schlotze,* Festwochen, Berlin
*Armpit,* Liverpool Biennial, Liverpool, UK
*True Love IV — Mission to Venus,* Gwangju Biennale,
  Gwangju, South Korea
*Flaschomat,* Kunsthalle St. Gallen, St. Gallen,
  Switzerland
*Grand Marquis,* Ars Futura Galerie, Zurich,
  Switzerland

**2001**

*Gelatin Is Getting It All Wrong Again,* Leo Koenig Inc.,
  New York
*Die Totale Osmose,* 49th Venice Biennale,
  Austrian Pavilion, Venice, Italy
*You Must Stop Curien!,* Sonsbeek 9: Locus/Focus,
  Arnhem, Netherlands
*Schlund,* Marstall, Munich, Germany
*Furball, Playing Amongst the Ruins,* Royal College
  of Art Galleries, London

**2000**

*A Hole to China,* 2000 Awesome Festival, Perth,
  Australia
*Kolibri d'amour, In the Beginning Was Merz — from
  Kurt Schwitters to the Present Day,* Sprengel
  Museum, Hannover, Germany
*Lebt und arbeitet in Wien,* Kunsthalle Vienna, Austria
*Buttik Transportør,* Galerie Meyer Kainer, Vienna,
  Austria

*Weltwunder, In Between,* EXPO 2000, Hannover,
  Germany
*The B-thing,* Lower Manhattan Cultural Council,
  World Trade Center, New York
*Das Ks Ks, Milch vom Ultrablauen Strom,* Kunsthalle
  Krems, Krems, Austria

**1999**

*Schlammloch,* Alhambra, Diendorf, Austria
*Hugbox,* Liverpool Biennial, Liverpool, UK
*The Gelatin Paprika Ship,* Bishopsgate Goodsyard,
  London
*Pollo Feliz,* Wahlverwandtschaften, Wiener
  Festwochen, Vienna, Austria
*Breakfast in Bed,* Austrian Cultural Institute, London
*Que Quapo!,* La Panaderia, Mexico City
*Human Elevator,* with Cargnelli/Szely, Mackie
  Apartment, Los Angeles, California
*I Like My Job II,* Royal College of Art, London

**1998**

*Abgasblase,* Schindlerhouse, Los Angeles, California
*Suck and Blow,* Spencer Brownstone Gallery,
  New York
*Percutaneous Delights,* P.S.1 Contemporary
  Art Center, New York

**1997**

*America,* Journey and Video Project, Miami;
  Memphis; Chattanooga; New York
*Association of Anonymous Astronauts,* with Bruno
  Stubenrauch, Public Netbase, Vienna, Austria
*Overdub,* Kunsthaus Glarus, Glarus, Switzerland
*Gelatins Little Spanking Show,* Flex, Vienna, Austria
*Truck High,* Journey and Performance, various
  highways, Austria
*Take the Elevator to the 3rd Floor,* Safe, New York

**1996**

*Junge Szene 1996,* Secession, Vienna, Austria
*Coming Up,* Museum Moderner Kunst–Stiftung
  Ludwig, 20er Haus, Vienna, Austria
*Pronoia in Exnerland,* Kunsthalle Exnergasse,
  Vienna, Austria

Published on the occasion
of the exhibition:

**Gelitin's Sweatwat**
Service Complet
October 17–October 21, 2005
from 6pm until 11pm
Exhibition: October 22 – November 26, 2005

Gagosian Gallery
6–24 Britannia Street
London, WC1X 9JD
T. 020.7841.9960
www.gagosian.com

Sweatwat Publication © 2006 Gagosian Gallery

SWEATWAT…Once a Noun, now a Verb
© 2006 Cerith Wyn Evans
Puddle Trouble: *Sweatwat* at King's Cross
© 2006 Claire Bishop

All artworks © Gelitin

Editors
Stefan Ratibor, Kay Pallister and Alison McDonald

Copy Editors
Nicole Heck and Donald Kennison

Photography of the artworks and installation by Gelitin,
Andre Ainsworth and Prudence Cuming Associates Ltd.
Images coordinated by Becky Poostchi.

Gelitin would like to thank
Cerith Wyn Evans, Sara Glaxia, Cosmo, Anthony Auerbach,
René Schweiger, Günther Bernhart, Christian Wurzer,
Rita Nowak, Darren Van-Asten, John Devolle, Shoko Arriba,
Alex Guri, Karen Breneman and Thomas Sandbichler.

Gagosian Gallery Sweatwat crew
Malena Bach, Roderick Barton, Roxana Bruno, Ian Cooke,
Hanna Freeberg, Philip Hausmeiser, Kay Pallister, James
Rawlinson, Andrew Stramentov and Gary Waterston.

Catalogue design
Christoph Steinegger/Interkool

Reproductions
Appel Grafik

Printed by Langebartels & Jürgens



ISBN # 1-932598-31-6

48